# The Jael Finishing School for Ladies

*Etiquette for Dangerous Women*

Jaime Hope McArdle

ISBN 978-1-0980-8871-2 (paperback)
ISBN 978-1-0980-8872-9 (digital)

Christian Faith Publishing, Inc.
832 Park Avenue
Meadville, PA 16335
www.christianfaithpublishing.com

Printed in the United States of America

But Jael the wife of Heber took a tent peg, and took a hammer in her hand. Then she went softly to him and drove the peg into his temple until it went down into the ground while he was lying fast asleep from weariness. So he died. And behold, as Barak was pursuing Sisera, Jael went out to meet him and said to him, "Come, and I will show you the man whom you are seeking." So he went in to her tent, and there lay Sisera dead, with the tent peg in his temple.

—Judges 4:21–22 (ESV)

# Prologue

During the time Deborah was judge of Israel, the people had turned from God and were cruelly oppressed by King Jabin for twenty years. Deborah would sit under a palm tree where people would come to her for judgment. One day the God of Israel spoke to Deborah and told her it was time to overthrow the oppressive reign of Jabin. She sent for Barak and instructed him to gather his men, draw out Sisera, the general of Jabin's army, and God would ensure his victory.

Barak said he would do this but only if Deborah would accompany him to the battle. She agreed but told Barak that because of this request, the glory of conquest would not go to him, instead Sisera would be delivered into the hands of a woman.

The men of Israel marched to draw out Sisera and the army of King Jabin, and God went before his people and routed the great army and all his chariots by the sword, but Sisera escaped the battle on foot and, seeking a place to hide, found himself at the tent of Jael, the wife of Heber the Kenite. There had been peace between King Jabin and Heber the Kenite, so Sisera felt safe there.

Jael beckoned Sisera into the tent, gave him a skin of milk to refresh him, and hid him under a rug. He instructed her to keep watch for him while he rested, but instead of obeying Sisera, the general of her people's oppressor, she took a tent peg and a hammer in her hand and softly went to Sisera and drove the tent peg into his temple until it went down to the ground while he slept. And so he died.

Jael then went out and found Barak who was pursuing Sisera and said to him, "Come, I will show you the man whom you are seeking," and led him to where Sisera lay dead with the tent peg in his temple.

So on that day, God subdued Jabin, the King of Canaan, before the people of Israel who had harshly oppressed them for twenty years. And the people of Israel continued to press harder and harder against Jabin until they destroyed his reign and won their freedom.

# Introduction

This story—like much of the Bible—isn't for the faint of heart. There is so much to unearth about women and the complex role we are called to. First thing to consider is *it was during the time Deborah was judge of Israel.* To understand this era, we will need some backstory.

This is the era of judges. Almost everyone has heard the story of Moses: the plagues on Egypt, "Let my people go," the Ten Commandments, the burning bush. If you missed the stories in Sunday school, they've worked their way into popular culture and movies enough to be familiar on some level.

To fill in some gaps, God's chosen people—when it was really just a large family—were living out a widespread famine in Egypt way, way, way back. At the time, they were a great help to Pharaoh because God had given a heads-up to one of his people, Joseph, that the famine was coming with enough lead time to prepare. Egypt had enough food to thrive in a desperate time, and Joseph, son of Jacob, ended up the equivalent to the prime minister of Egypt. The people God brought there were successful and grew into a nation within a nation. However, over time, new leaders came to power that forgot how those people of God (the nation of Israel, what we today call Jews) had saved the country and made it rich, grew fearful of their success and numbers, and began to turn against them.

Over time, the Jews became slaves in Egypt, but God did not forget them. In fact, much like Joseph's personal enslavement story, they continued to have God's favor, and the nation of Israel grew even in oppression. This made the rulers of Egypt devise a plan to kill all the boys who were born for a time in order to control the population. There was one woman in particular who had the courage to hide her little son and then take him to the Nile River and set him afloat in a basket in the hope that somehow he might survive. What a crazy plan! He could have been crocodile food or drown, but God had a purpose for this little one, and he was picked up by an Egyptian princess and raised as her own in the palace. We know him as Moses. And not only did he survive, he was educated in the palace as a prince and became the one God used to set his people free.

When the time was right, Moses brought the people who were in generations of slavery out of Egypt. This is a fascinating story of God versus the powers of darkness. Moses, as the representative of God, went head-to-head with Pharaoh, the evil king of Egypt who the prince of darkness was using to keep God's people in chains. You definitely should read the backstory if you haven't. It starts in Exodus (as in the exit out of slavery in Egypt) God brought the people out of Egypt, but the people refused to allow God to get the Egypt out of them. That transition was difficult and meant a lot of lessons in the wilderness such that only two men from the original population God delivered saw the entry to the promised land (Joshua and Caleb).

The next generation born in the wilderness, born in freedom, came into the promised land one parcel at a time under the leadership of Joshua. God was clear that he was raising up a nation to represent him to the world. God could have sent the angel of death on ahead and cleared out the place for the people to move on in, but that would have left his people weak and shallow. They were only one generation from slave mentality. God wanted people who stood tall and walked into their freedom and had strength and light for the world. He made it clear that he would train them to take the land one territory at a time, and he would leave some of the inhabitants for a time in order to work the land not yet taken so it didn't go to a wasteland but also to use them to train his people to have courage and to partner with God to fight for freedom and justice. We can see in reading that God's people had lots of flaws and weakness, and the enemy civilizations were also used to give the people of Israel times of check and balance and put them into a time-out when they strayed.

Farther back in Genesis, there is a passage I find fascinating. While God is talking to Abraham (the father of the nation of Israel) about what will happen to his future generations, He tells a story of a people who wander in the land that is not their own and then become servants (slaves) for four hundred years, but someday they will return to the land promised to be their home—in the fourth generation "for the iniquity of the Amorites is not yet complete." There is much we do not understand about God's plan, but he told Abraham, generations in advance, that his chosen people would grow into a nation under oppression, and he would not set them free until the evil of the people in the land came to a fullness that brought judgment upon them.

Something we don't seem to contextualize as a modern Western culture is that many of our basic tenants are based on the laws God gave to his people. We value life and have laws that protect it. We have a justice system and fight against oppression. Though the humans in these systems create lots of complication and problems, we struggle with greed and power-hungry individuals, the basic ideals we uphold are sanctity of life, freedom, and justice.

The cultures of other ancient civilizations were not based on freedom and justice. They lived with pagan rituals that used women (and boys and men) in their temples as prostitutes, and their custom was human sacrifice (children mostly) in the fire to their own gods. God created humans in His own image and demands that all lives are worthy of honor and respect. Yet he also gives us all the choice to decide for ourselves: choose life or choose death. The attitude of "do whatever feels good and makes you happy" way of life usually ends up hurting and dehumanizing people around you. This sickens God to the heart. He allowed these cultures to continue until their time of living in this horrific way was "complete." It seems likely he also gave them time to change their ways and make a better choice. When they didn't, and time was up, he brought his people to come in to bring judgment and take back the land. The instructions for the chosen people were to live in the way that honored God and the people around them and choose differently from the destructive and selfish cultures in ancient times. The Ten Commandments, which are based on life having dignity and honoring your neighbor as yourself, were radically different from the ancient way of life in the era.

As long as the people of Israel were close to God and allowed him to be king of their lives and their nation, God blessed them and protected them. They were a light to the other nations of how a people should live, honoring God who created them and each other. It seemed that whenever they got too comfortable, they would stray and get distracted and begin to dabble or dive into things that would destroy them. God's laws and rules were not random. He created the universe. And he knew that if they took the paths of evil, it would lead to their own demise, pain, and death. When he punished them, it was to help them come back to their freedom and life.

There is a way that seems right to a man,
but in the end, it leads to death. (Proverbs 14:12)

During this first period of taking over the land, the nation of Israel was directly under God. He was their King. He gave them his rules and went with them. He fought in their battles, and he spoke to their leaders. He set judges in place to help solve disputes and direct foreign affairs. He had prophets (both men and women) he spoke with directly to help guide the people. During the story of Jael and Sisera, we read that it was a time that Deborah was a prophet and judge of Israel. This tells us the main leader of the nation of Israel at the time and the one God spoke most directly to was a woman. A woman, under God himself, led the nation at a critical time.

Many people incorrectly assume that Christianity and following the God of the Bible is either antiwoman or oppressive to women. As in any book, passages can be taken out of context and used by people to oppress others and push their own agendas. They will be successful to the extent the ones they seek to oppress and convince know the truth. If one were to study the entire Bible texts without bias, one would see evidence that God champions women time after time and intends for men and women to work together in complimentary roles. Sometimes women were put in vitally important positions where nations hinged on their strength, and this story is one of those examples.

The people had turned to evil, and God sold them back into oppression for a time. Think of it like a time-out to stop, reconsider your choices, and make better ones. What happened when the people turned to evil is they forgot who they were. They were chosen to be God's representatives to the world. This meant they needed to live differently than the cultures around them. This was truly their one job—just get this right: love God with your whole self. Build your culture on justice for the poor, love the people around you, and consider life sacred. Honor your parents, care for the young, and treat foreigners in the nation with dignity and friendship. Do not worship money, power, yourself, but instead turn to God who cares for you and provides all good things. Learn his laws, and then keep them because they bring life and honor. Be a shining light of how to live well.

This particular time-out was about twenty years. God decided their punishment was done. This might have been about how long it took for them to feel enough discomfort to want to stop trying their own ways that led to destruction and begin to seek God and ask for him to intervene.

This is where the story of Deborah and Jael picks up.

# Chapter 1

# Boot Camp

I never heard the story of Jael as a little girl in Sunday school. (I can imagine why not.) I don't remember it from summer Bible camp either. Once I came into adulthood, when the story is more age-appropriate, I had quit seeking the Bible as my road map and had securely locked Jesus in the trunk. A couple years ago when I realized I had gotten so off track, I was lost beyond my understanding and almost plunged off some cliffs. I began digging for a better navigation system. I did an audio Bible from Genesis to Revelation, desperate for insight. So I'm certain the story was included, but I did not particularly remember it.

For as many people I've met who have a Bible, or know it exists, and who think they know what it contains, sadly, fewer have opened one up and read much of it for themselves. I am still finding new layers in the stories and am amazed with continual new insights, lessons, and layers each time I open mine. There is no book like it in the world. It is as close as we come to real magic, a living text that upon opening, you never really know what will leap out, grab hold of you, shift your thinking and, sometimes, your very life. It is like a pair of glasses—it's not for looking at, it's for looking through. Digging into the Bible brings life around you into focus. And once you can see through truth and it all begins to make sense, you wonder why other people still bump into things and walk around in confusion. The glasses are free (at least in this country at the time of this writing) for the taking. And once you are able to navigate with less damage, you can't imagine going back.

It is one of the most dangerous books in print in that way. Why else is it so controversial? Why else do so many people own a copy but never open it? Why else are there deep unseen powers working overtime to ensure humans are adequately distracted by anything else—work commitments, family responsibilities, more sleep, parties and friends, alcohol and drugs, shopping, eating, traveling, social media, binge-watching TV episodes? The best way for the jailer of the dark places to keep people in confusion is to distract with "good" things. The things that occupy our time can be so deceptive.

There seems to be a formula ensuring that people have at least one Bible or, even better, a collection of them on a shelf somewhere yet no time to open one and if the time does present. The second barrier is to feel overwhelmed by where and how to begin. In places where the dangerous living book is outright banned, people risk their lives to pass around small sections and chapters from within it and read it as if their very lives depend on it—usually memorizing as much as possible because merely possessing the writings can mean imprisonment. Literally hiding the words in their hearts, they forgo sleeping and eating to get a taste of what the pages hold. It brings light into dark places and life into dead things. They have felt its power.

It is most often not until we find ourselves in our own dark and dead place and have tried almost everything else that, in desperation, we begin to get serious about this search.

It was during my years of great struggle that I read Judges 4, and the story came off the page in a new dimension.

It was the culminating hard year following many challenging ones. Looking back, it was the most difficult year I've faced. The future I had envisioned, which was built on shaky foundations of shifting sand, was dissolving into a black hole and seemed threatening to suck me away with it as well.

I knew deep down that God was leading me through dark hallways out of the prison I'd navigated myself into and that it was his will alone that kept me from being sucked into the vortex of nothingness that was taking much of my life as I knew it. Two things I now realize in hindsight: I only lost what was necessary to walk into healing and wholeness; and I could never lose myself or what truly matters because I belong to the one who made me, and he holds it all together in his hands.

There seems to be a moment in the crack of the day—that little fleeting moment between waking and sleeping, a moment when the spiritual and the physical seems like a feather's touch, a baton being passed from one state to the next in the spirit. That moment has brought messages of deep meaning. Great insights have come in those seconds before I am fully awake to the day.

One morning in the middle of the year of great struggle—during the week I had read the story of Jael, Deborah, Barak, and Sisera—I woke up with the thought that I was in training. This was my boot camp year.

I began a mostly awake conversation with the whisper in my spirit:

> WHISPER. You are in finishing school.
>
> ME. That's a strange way to see it. Finishing school is a place where you learn things like serving high tea, make pleasant innocuous conversation, to carry yourself with correct posture, and become a lady. I feel like I'm being held underwater until I think I might die and then pulled out, tossed onto shore, and then sent hiking, soaking wet, and cold up the mountain barefoot, shot at, duck for cover, then run back down again to repeat it all the next day, bruised and bloody but somehow still alive.
>
> WHISPER. That is because this is the Jael finishing school for ladies. It is where you learn what is necessary to become a freedom-fighter.
>
> ME. Explain.
>
> WHISPER. You are a daughter of the Creator, King of the universe, the one who commands the angel armies.

You have been chosen and brought into his royal family. You are now princess *and* warrior. You must learn peace, diplomacy, beauty, sacrifice, and service along with the weapons of war to defeat the powers of darkness around you. You are in both boot camp and finishing school at the same time. Think of it as the Jael Finishing School for Ladies.

ME. That does sound like the experience my life has become lately.

WHISPER. It would make a fantastic book title too, would it not?

ME (Laughing out loud while getting up from my bed to start the day). Yes, it would.

# Chapter 2

# Danger to the Gates of Hell

I t is never too soon to consider what your life is about. At some point, you will come to the end of it, and you cannot know when that day will arrive. When that day comes, I imagine we will all ask in that instant: What did it amount to? If the stories of your life do flash before your eyes at your last moments this side of eternity, what will matter when you consider it all?

I have a favorite quote by Andy Stanley: "If you live your life only for yourself, at the end of your life, you will only have yourself to show for yourself."

At some point in the year of great struggle, I asked myself: What am I doing here? Is it all meaningless? What is my purpose? When I get to the end of my life, what do I hope to look back and see my life was about?

I had always wanted a meaningful life. In high school, I thought that would come with being the best or in an upper tier in a field—success. I decided against going into music as a major study because I knew I was average at best in playing the violin. Then I decided, at least, having work that mattered: an engineer to create useful things, a medical professional who would save lives, any career that had a vital impact on lives. I struggled deeply with my passion for music and the fact that I might not be incredibly successful or have much useful impact on the world yet that seemed to be what I was constantly being steered toward in all the signs around me.

Finally in midcollege, I was given the most memorable advice of my life from a beloved violin teacher who was one of the smartest people I knew (she had a complicated science degree from Yale) and a gifted musician (with a master's degree from Eastman School of Music). Teresa Ling was a mentor and friend who I still know and value today for a life lived with grace and honor. As I laid out my struggle, she said, "Jaime, you do not have to be the best musician in your field. You only have to find your place, your niche, where you belong, and only you can fill. Then you have a meaningful career and life."

Those words struck me deeply, and I changed my major to violin performance. I became a teacher with some gift at helping people grow in their violin study and encouraging them in their lives as well. Yet I still struggled to feel my life made a true difference in the world. I saw music as a superfluous luxury, not a vital part of life. I was part of the entertainment world. Indeed, entertainment is positive. But I'm a serious person! I want to have value in the essential category. I kept this low-grade concern at bay, knowing that with teaching, I directly impacted young lives and cared about them. And that must be at least more than entertainment.

When I realized that there was more to life than what we see on the surface, and no matter what our physical world job is, we are engaged in an epic of struggle of light and darkness. It changed how I saw my career. I began to realize that my job was only one way I interacted in this larger truth.

In asking the question after this new understanding, I thought a moment, and then I came up with the only thing that seemed worth living for anymore: I want to be a danger to the gates of hell.

And I tell you, you are Peter. And on this
rock, I will build my church, and the gates of hell
shall not prevail against it. (Matthew 16:18 ESV)

Jesus spoke of the gates of hell. Gates are defensive. They keep things both in and out; they protect something behind them. If the gates cannot prevail, that means they will eventually fail. And the church itself is what he tells us breaks through. This means the church is intended to be on offense against the gates of hell, not defense. We have a serious problem with the church in the western cultural world today. Many churches in comfortable countries are playing defense, trying to fight back the attacks of darkness. We are putting out fires instead of starting them. What we seek are happy little lives where we can live in the blessings of God and keep our families safe, where we make an unspoken truce with the darkness: I won't have a lot of impact on the world around me if you leave me alone here to enjoy my life. Give me successful work, and please don't touch my family.

Many things could go wrong with that way of living. It deceptively feels safe because the agents of darkness *do* have a lot of freedom to operate in this fallen world. Since we are all in enemy territory, it can seem like a good diplomatic play to opt for a peace treaty with the ruling forces. But the agents of darkness only lie, steal, kill, and destroy. They are not honorable. And once you make the deal, you begin to live double-minded. You aren't really honest with God anymore because you have this other life you know isn't really right, so you lose the close intimate connection that you need most, living in enemy territory. And what you gain is a treaty that is fated to be broken but probably only when you've almost completely lost the lifeline you'll need to survive the attack when it does come.

Even worse, you don't realize that is what you're doing. It seems harmless, one step at a time into the double life, until you don't recognize truth anymore for what it is. This is how we get to the end of our life and then wonder, What was it all about: living safe, finding my own happiness, protecting my family?

Or maybe you are built more like me. And the answers look like taking on challenges, finding my limits, working harder and longer than others, being the best I can be at whatever I did, taking risks to get what I want, setting and accomplishing goals, allowing nothing to stand in my way.

Is that really what life is about? Because it's still all about me. I'm singing my favorite song all my life long—"me, me, me, meeeeee!"

I pondered how hollow in the end that would be. I can tell myself that I'm doing good things, it's good to become the best version of myself. I was engaged in creating a nonprofit strings education program that allowed access to kids of all financial and education backgrounds. I was performing and sharing music. I was on local arts boards and volunteering time when I was able. I was riding horses long distances and encouraging those around me whenever I could. Why did it still feel hollow?

*Only myself to show for myself.*

I came to see that I was working hard and doing good things, but I was doing the things that interested me and offering them to God as what I wanted my life to be about. What he required of me was to lay all of that at his feet and ask him: What would you have me do?

The Creator King made me unique, and he knows better than I do of what will be fulfilling, effective, and where my particular skills are needed. No one else on the planet can do what I'm called to do. Thankfully, many things he had written into my heart were already moving forward. Even from the trunk where I had tried to keep him out of the driver seat, he is—God. Even from the trunk, he is ultimately in control. He prefers our cooperation and love. He has great patience, but he also has plans way bigger than I could have dreamed up on my own.

If I only offered what my human self was capable of, it would be small in the end. In fact, God says it's really garbage in comparison. If I threw it all on the ground at his feet and asked him to sort it out then reorganize my entire life and empower me to do things he wanted me to do and to go places he wanted me to go, well that's a life that has the potential to get the attention of the very forces of hell. You cannot help but make an impact when you let God make the plan. The more of the plan you give up and accept from him, the bigger the impact and the bigger the adventure. It can be frightening to look into that unknown and agree to go, not knowing what you're even agreeing to.

As C. S. Lewis writes in the Chronicles of Narnia, "No, he is not tame! He is wild. But he is good."

When you come to that place, laying the good (and not so good) things you've been busy with at his feet and asking him to sort them out and then give you the plan, buckle up. It's going to get wild.

The sooner you consider what you want your life to mean, the better. It may change through seasons, but don't procrastinate. Be honest. For a long time, I wanted to live my life for myself, and deep down, I knew it. I didn't want to face that truth and see my life for the basically selfish endeavor it was. Sometimes I have to pray that God will help me *want* to *want* what is best for me when I know it's not really where I am yet.

Sometimes I have to pray to *want* the courage to go where I'm called to go and do what I'm called to do. The current is pulling everyone along regardless if we want it to or not. We are never treading water or standing still, we are going somewhere each day. We are either pulled along by the current of the culture around us, or we begin to swim in an intentional direction against that current. Floating along in the current is easy. Most everyone floats along together. Once in a while, someone rolls through our lives, swimming against the current. It looks hard, and most people can't understand why one would bother. Swimming takes strength. Often as we watch their lives, we admire something about them and their determination. We can all do it, but getting somewhere intentionally takes decision, commitment, and discipline. The choice is yours.

# Chapter 3

# Warrior Prince

I had made my truce with the dark side, not wanting to read the fine print. Can I claim ignorance if the ignorance is intentional? As with all prisoners of this war, I went willingly. At first I was drawn by the promises of fun, happiness, pleasure, and getting to live for myself. Though I would have never admitted it directly, I wanted to be my own god. I wanted to decide what I would do, when I would do it, and who I would do it with. "This is true freedom," the velvet voice of the darkness would murmur in my ear. True freedom means being your own god. It's the same story he gave Eve.

The enemy of our hearts is not creative. He doesn't have to be. We all are tempted by the same basic thing, the lie that we should be the god of our own lives. It never stops there. We begin to want to be the god to those around us as well. We see it everywhere as people strive to get their own way, then to get people around them to do what they want by lying, cheating, manipulating, passive-aggressive behavior, or forcing with violence and abuse. How often is it "for their own good"? It seems harmless in the beginning. We want to live our own lives. But that dark seed grows into trying to get everyone around us to do what is right in our own eyes as well. We become the judge for ourselves and others.

A deeply twisted example of this is called tolerance, in the case where one insists they accept everyone as they are. They proudly declare all people and cultures to have the ability to decide for themselves. They only do not accept the people who do not agree with their enlightened tolerance view and would like to force those bad "intolerant" people to line up with their own ideals. The darkness is not creative, but it is very tricky. When we sit in darkness, we are easily convinced that evil is good. In fact, most of the worst things humans do to one another come from a place of believing they are right and only have the best in mind, from broken friendships to world wars.

> Woe to those who call evil good and good evil, who put darkness for light and light for darkness, who put bitter for sweet and sweet for bitter! Woe to those who are wise in their own eyes and shrewd in their own sight! (Isaiah 5:20–21 ESV)

> For although they knew God, they did not honor him as God or give thanks to him, but they became futile in their thinking, and their foolish hearts were darkened. Claiming to be wise, they became fools. (Romans 1:21–22 ESV)

Deep down while I languished in my own prison, I knew something wasn't right. Not every day but at certain points, truth would waft up from somewhere like a breeze. I was created for freedom. I was made to feel the sun on my skin and walk without chains. Once you've been in there long enough though, you can't imagine what it would take to get out. Then there's the fact that you went willingly and embraced it. You were promised things, and you don't have them yet. You may have things actually, you may have the family you wanted, the success you'd hoped for, the money to live comfortably—if you do, it's likely you are stalked by the fear that one false move will shatter the glass house you've built. The satisfaction, peace, and fullness of life you crave isn't there, and you're sure it will be if you only stick around a little longer. If you don't have it, then it's always right around the corner, just a little farther down the path. Keep on, and either way, it's best not to think too deeply about it.

The agents of darkness use tactics unique to each person to keep you in your own individual prison. Free will is real. The bottom line is you can only be lured by the darkness—never taken by force. They don't even have the keys to their own kingdom. So deception, empty promise, threats, fear, and pain are the only tools they have. And they are masters at them. Most of us go so willingly—it only takes the right bait.

God loves the world and all the people that he created. It breaks his heart to see us all in these prisons, so he wrote himself into the story. He showed up behind enemy lines, hiding his birth in a little barn stall. He did crazy subversive activities like forgiving people and healing them even on holy days. The religious leaders were beside themselves: This man was breaking the rules! He did so much good he had to be taken out. He is the biggest danger to the gates of hell of all. We read that he allowed himself to be caught, tortured, unjustly tried, and killed in the worst way the Roman Empire was executing (maybe except being fed to a lion, that sounds pretty bad to me too). And in doing so, he was taken to the heart of hell, and the prince of darkness danced and celebrated the victory, certain he'd finally conquered once and for all—game over. Humans now have no hope.

But no! The story doesn't end there. Triumphantly, from the worst possible scenario came the best possible outcome. Our warrior prince hero came out of the prisons of hell with the keys in hand. It is said the power was so strong on the earth when the resurrection of God's Son himself came to pass, that the dead in faith all over the area came out of their graves and walked among the living.

> The tombs also were opened, and many bodies of the saints who had fallen asleep were raised, and coming out of the tombs after his resurrection, they went into the holy city and appeared to many. (Matthew 27:52–53 ESV)

I can't even imagine one of those personal stories. Your father who died in an accident two years ago comes in the front door after the resurrection. The grave couldn't hold him. There are so many side stories from a verse here and there I wonder about. No wonder this little sect of Jesus's followers grew against all odds in that first century when the man who has spent three years making the blind see, the deaf hear, the dumb speak, and the dead live tells his followers in as plain Aramaic as he can, "I will die and in three days rise again," then he dies in a public execution in front of anyone with the stomach to watch (in the manner he also predicted), and the sun goes black when his spirit leaves his body, a great earthquake comes and the massive separation in the temple is ripped *from the top down* as if God himself tore it in two, shows back up alive to hundreds of people after three days, and to top it off, the power of resurrection is so intense that others who believed in this God of the Jews *came out of their graves* walking through town alive again. Threats from the Roman Empire to kill anyone who follows this way ring hollow. Not even death can stop a movement like that. Of course, they were bold. Of course, they had no fear of hell or the Roman Empire. These were free men and women.

The hero we all have been hungering for—the hero of every fairy tale, every action-adventure movie, every woman's deepest heart's desire—is the warrior prince who would fight through the very gates of hell to bring us home. Why is the hunger for that so deeply instilled into every heart? Because it is true. Somewhere in the deepest places, it is a tiny seed throbbing and begging for light, air, and water so it can come alive. It is true. The warrior King has come and fought through hell to bring us out. Still we cower in the dark, afraid of what will happen if we try the door.

This King is Creator, guide, Father and beloved. He is both lion and lamb. He is all of this at once and more. I mix my imagery from time to time on purpose because for some it is a season where what is yearned for is a strong father who will scoop up a lost child to safety and provide everything needed, for some it is the friend closer than a brother who gives the best advice and walks through life together, and for others it is the beloved, a true heart who will fight through hell itself to be reunited with the other heart that beats as one with his own. He is. He is everything at once. Even if we humans cannot comprehend and have to switch back and forth like a cubist, painting to try to grasp the facets of an all-encompassing God.

Can you imagine the broken heart of that Creator, Father, King, warrior, best friend, beloved, prince as he calls to each of us from the other side of the door? To him we are his child, brother, sister, princess, beloved, queen, and he is desperate to regain your heart to safety. Relationships are two-sided. I think we get stuck in our human construct imagining that we need God, but why would God need us? He is God, complete, has it all in one. Yet if that were true, why bother with all this—wipe us out in mercy and maybe start over again? Miraculously, it is the depth of his love for us that stands on the other side of the door in blood and tears. He is not unaffected by us. He is desperate to free us and bring us home. He is relentless in his pursuit of us, like the hero's words as the beloved is being led away to captivity: I will find you! His determination is unstoppable—almost. The only one who can stop him from bringing us home is us.

In the same way we walked into the prison willingly, we must desire our own freedom, we must want to come out. He waits with tears of grief like a father who desperately wants to see a child released from captivity, eyes burning for the beloved he's given so much to find.

"I am here waiting to lead you through the dark hallways to safety. I won't let you down, but I can't force you to come. I've given my own life to do this—just try the door. The door locks only from the inside. You have to unlock it yourself. You must desire your own freedom. If you don't have the strength to open the door, unlock it. Call to me, and I will come in and get you. Can you hear me? I'm right here. *Can you hear me?*"

There finally came a day when, close to death in my soul, I began to move. For me it was 2:00 a.m., and I couldn't sleep from the heaviness of death in my heart. I sat on the floor of my living room in the most despair I've ever felt. And the only line I could write over and over in my journal for two pages with tears in my eyes was *No one can help me. No one.*

The death was in my spirit. And though I have never been one to seriously consider killing my body, this was one time where I hoped somehow I would simply cease to exist because breathing became too much effort. What brought me here was the end of myself and my own plans. I had made "good things" my "ultimate things" as Tim Keller explains. And God had not allowed me to have what I had done everything in my own human-manipulating heart to get. I believed if I had this one more thing, then I would be okay. My life would not be hollow. I would finally be happy, have peace and joy. But it was a lie. And in his mercy, God blocked me from what I thought would finally give my life meaning. As the darkness closed in on my prison, I felt I would surely die.

Sometimes God allows us to have the thing we believe our identities and egos will be satisfied with. And when that too turns up hollow, many find themselves on top of the very mountain they set out to conquer alone and in the dark. We are created to find our fullness and abundance in intimacy with him and living out God's purpose for us, and we will never be satisfied with the cheap trinkets we think will fill us. For those who come to a real dead end in either case, we have a choice.

That night I had only enough strength to crawl through the mud toward the door. I reached for the lock. I wasn't even sure if I had been able to reach the latch before I collapsed again on the ground covered in mud.

# Chapter 4

# The Healing

The next thing, I saw only in an impression months later on a solo retreat to my favorite B and B in Coastal Virginia. I spend a few days each year for my birthday on the streams, inlets, and rivers near the Chesapeake Bay on a standing paddle board talking to and listening to God. One morning, out on the glassy streams, I had a mental view of the door of that prison cell being pushed open. As I lay lifeless, the warrior prince lifted me out of the mud. Being out of my mind completely, I began scratching and tearing at my hero as he, without hesitation, continued to carry me through the dark hallways, climbing out of the hell I had found myself. In confusion, I screamed and fought, drawing blood. But it was too late. I had unlocked the door and called for help. So now in spite of myself, I was going to come alive. The open air stung in my lungs, and the light was so bright I was blinded for a time. I began to go through the process of being washed clean. It isn't enough to get out of Egypt as the song goes, it took time to get the Egypt out of me. Instead of life, it felt like death. But I was too weak to protest anymore and fell heavy into his arms to be brought to my real home to learn the truth of who I really am. This was only the beginning.

In case I mislead anyone to thinking this is an overnight process, from the night I began to make a move for the door until I woke up in a place to begin healing was over two years. Even when I began to move in the dark, I went in circles, found other walls first. I still tried to do it on my own at times, not willing to give up completely to another. Maybe I can retain partial control? Still my hero never gave up on me, even through the waiting, for me to find enough will to keep moving toward his voice. He kept calling to me even when I'd get tangled up in the wrong direction. His voice, calm and steady, kept me alive and encouraged me to keep trying.

Looking back, I know I had been almost mortally wounded. I found myself spiritually in intensive care, so to speak, with deep wounds, eyes that couldn't handle the light, weak from malnutrition and dehydration, muscles unable to steady myself on my own. As I continued to revive completely—bathing in the words and support of strong prayer and support all around me—I would take two steps and fall on my face, trying out my new found strength, weak as it was, and all the while crying out, "Send me in! I am ready! There are people still in there!"

The great physician of the heart was kind to me. In his love, he locked me in my recovery garden sanctuary, and I submitted to the healing process.

"You are not ready," he would say. "But let's work on this for now."

And he would give me little assignments I could handle to keep the stir crazy at bay. Most of the healing process was painful, yet I demanded the fast track so it was one wave after another with as little time in between as I could stand. I had a dream before the process began where I was in a long line of people who wanted a word from "the Father." And as it was my turn, he said to me, "You are doing well, I am pleased. If you could go any faster, you would."

I held onto these words constantly in that difficult time.

His compassion was tender. As I grew stronger, I was able to walk in the gardens of my sanctuary with Him as we talked about my wounds, how the healing of them would take place. I spent many hours facing the decisions that had taken me into the dark prison, things I did that hurt myself and people around me. Yet after each excruciating session of pulling the vines and weeds from my heart, roots, and all, this is a painful process if it's done right. He always brought the balm of grace and love to turn with healing waters the newly exposed soil into something rich and beautiful.

In this season, forgiveness was the assignment of highest importance and learning to put to death the things I thought would bring me life but were lies. There was a vivid early morning, barely conscious scene, when I knew I was being called to do something difficult, something important to me I had to release forever was only hours away. I had that whisper between the worlds.

I saw Jesus bruised and bloody, carrying a crossbeam, walking by me in my barely conscious mind. He looked at me and said, "Come."

I stayed frozen in place.

> ME. I can't. It's too much for me. I can't do it.
> WHISPER. You can. I will be with you.
> ME. It is death. I'm terrified. This will kill me.
> WHISPER. I know that is what it appears. I promise you can trust me.
> ME. I don't have your strength.
> WHISPER. You do. I live in you now.
> ME. Okay. I will try.

And in that impression in my mind, I put one foot in front of the other to follow Jesus to certain death. To my amazement, when we arrived, it wasn't death but a garden. I was in a beautiful dress, and he was clean of all blood and in fresh clothes, and all around me was life and beauty.

> WHISPER. Do you still not understand? Do you doubt the depth of my love for you?

Truly that day, what I was called to do did feel like death. Yet also I knew when it was over that it was what had to be, and there were many smaller deaths I was called to walk into, each time bringing on the other side of it more life, a garden to heal in. I couldn't do it alone, but I had to participate. I had to choose, each time, to submit to the thing in front of me I was called to face. The deaths I had to walk through were about killing the lies and the things I had put my hopes for happiness and a fulfilling life in to put complete trust that God would decide what was best for my heart. Sometimes the thing was removed because it was damaging. Sometimes the thing was returned to me in a new way that didn't control me anymore but could be used for good. I didn't always know which it would be going in. But with each death I submitted to, my life grew stronger.

People who know me have asked how I seemed to go through this process in a relatively short amount of time (the bulk of it took about a year) and to come out whole and stronger instead of broken, wounded, and bitter. I know it was only because I finally called out to God and turned the entire process over to him from the depth and desperation of my heart. I believe everyone has a unique process. I tried everything on my own, everything that the world has to offer to get out of my prison, and only the resurrection power of God that brought the God-man out of hell produced a new life for me. That is the power. When we kill all the deeply entrenched self-centered ego parts of us, then a life is transformed from within. That makes us a danger to the gates of hell.

I understand why some turn to me and ask why I can't tone it down a little, the Jesus and Christian angle stuff. So many of these concepts could be done without expecting people to choose Jesus. And look how many more people I could help if I didn't turn off those who are adverse to a religion. Yes, I spent years here as well. It's nice to find some innocuous impersonal universe we can all agree on. Choose your own higher power, and let's all come together with what we do share. While you always have the right to choose your higher power, I cannot pretend they are all equal. And I cannot pretend they all offer equal freedom. I cannot because I've tried them, and I've watched others try them. It is true that the concepts of love and self-sacrifice and doing good make for a nicer prison cell than giving yourself entirely over to destruction of yourself and those around you, but it's still a prison. Sometimes it's worse because it's a nice prison, and you might even begin to think it's really the same as being free or actually better. I mean, you get three meals a day and a kind of protection you rationalize. Being out there in the real world is wild and dangerous. That's true too. I cannot know this fundamental thing and not speak it out of fear some will walk away. I cannot make that choice for them. I cannot water down where the power lies because it's more than some can handle. I cannot control that. It's insincere and deceptive to hide part of what I know especially if I think it's for someone's own good.

Have you ever asked yourself why the very name of Jesus is so controversial? If you speak of it as a person, you will likely be considered an extreme fanatic. Even those who are okay with a general God often draw the line when you want to bring in Jesus the God-man. Or they look at you with the recognition of a family member: "You too?"

It is the only name that has the healing power to change lives from the dark depths of the heart. I went through the hope that maybe "the universe" would intervene and do something nice for me. Friends suggested the teachings of Buddha. I tried many well-meaning human processes of working through pain and being a better person. These all spring from what I can do to keep control and do it myself. Chasing the wind is all that was in the end. None of it brought me freedom. There is a name that holds a power that makes darkness tremble. Try it sometime. Simply speaking that name creates a change in the atmosphere. It stirs up something like no other name or religious system or dead mystic leader will.

It was only because of this love that poured into my life from God that he sent his own warrior prince Son to hell and back for me that I could heal in the depths of my heart. It is only in facing the darkness within that we can ever face the darkness without. And we cannot face the darkness in ourselves honestly until we have the confidence of knowing that the very Creator King of the universe knows all of it and still chooses us. We can finally find our identity in the love he has for us. And only then, the deepest, darkest places cannot hold us anymore. Face them, expose them, and have no fear because he can bring us home and wash us clean. That is true freedom and healing, to be fully known and fully loved. That is what our hearts long for more than anything else in this world.

My healing came when I was willing to see the depth of my own depraved heart, taking responsibility for the part I had in the pain and facing the darkness hiding below. I heard it said that if you bear 1 percent responsibility for a thing, that makes you responsible. It gives very little room to pout over being a victim when you see this truth. This process of searching your heart with God's spotlight doesn't happen once and then it's over. It is like a washing the dust from our feet that we must do on a constant basis, asking for help from God and from close, trusted, like-minded friends to be shown where the infection begins to creep in.

> Examine me, God, and know my heart; test me, and know my thoughts! See if there is in me any hurtful way, and lead me along the eternal way. (Psalm 139:23–24 CJB)

I try to remember, every time I see something I dislike in people and circumstances around me, to go immediately to the mirror. Where can I find an example of it in my own heart? Ruthlessly, I ask for help, removing every plank I find in my own eyes, and allow God to work on the speck in other's lives. I think one needs to hear the audible voice of God before considering telling someone else their faults or at least the audible voice of the other person asking our view from the outside. Then if you aren't truly willing to lay down your life for that person, I suggest you still think twice before responding. Living in enemy territory, especially being a freedom fighter, is a dangerous business. As we go higher up on the list of those dangerous in the war, the tactics get more subversive and subtle. The enemy's plans even use our God-given righteousness and confidence against us and twist the very words of God to do things that hurt instead of heal. Being a freedom fighter requires ruthless self-seeking humility to root out any darkness that seeds into our hearts.

# Chapter 5

# Freedom Fighter

I considered what it meant that I wanted my life to be a danger to the gates of hell. For me it means to strike back at the evil forces that keep people in prisons. I had spent too much time as a prisoner of war, weak from malnourishment and lack of light. I couldn't wait to join the war against darkness. There were so many who needed to hear they too could walk out of their prison.

> Christ has set us free to live a free life. So take your stand! Never again let anyone put a harness of slavery on you. (Galatians 5:1 MSG)

As I began to find my strength, I kept begging to get to work.

ME. I'm ready. Send me in. I am going stir crazy here!
WHISPER. Patience.
ME. We're wasting time!
WHISPER. Great journeys with great purpose take great preparation.
ME. This is taking forever. People are dying out there!
WHISPER. Like a bow, you must be drawn back into strength and tension before you can be released effectively.
ME. I can hardly stand it. I have to find some darkness!

WHISPER. I cannot send you until the time is right. The casualties will be too great. You will be released when I know you will strategically hit exactly where I aim.

And so I continued in the Jael Finishing School for Ladies, learning the skills necessary to be released into the war that continues to rage. I desperately wanted to be a freedom fighter, yet I had much to learn. I had a lot of rough edges to get smoothed out before I could love well. I still have much to learn. I will be learning and learning until I am finished with my life here. The depths available are infinite, and the treasures available are unfathomable.

As I was immersed in the knowledge provided by the Creator King through my day-to-day schooling, I found a new understanding of myself and the world around me. I could remember, in times past, seeing behaviors and choices others made and even looking at myself in confusion, not understanding why things happened, why people did what they did, even why I did things I did, felt the way I felt, or ended up in places I ended up. Situations from strife amongst friends to world news and events began to take on a new clarity. It was like putting on glasses after spending years with blurred vision.

God wants us to have the understanding we need to navigate through enemy territory. He provided us a manual and navigation map that is a living guide. I realize many people avoid the manuals in our earthly lives. But in this case, it's life or death. And when we stray so far from our created purpose, eventual destruction of ourselves and those we care most about is highly likely.

Make me to know your ways, O, *Lord*; teach me your paths. (Psalm 25:4 ESV)

Your word is a lamp to my feet and a light to my path. (Psalm 119:105 ESV)

For the *Lord* gives wisdom; from his mouth come knowledge and understanding; guarding the paths of justice and watching over the way of

his people. Then you will understand righteousness and justice and equity, every good path; for
wisdom will come into your heart, and knowledge will be pleasant to your soul. (Proverbs 2:
6, 8–10)

I found a voracious hunger for the words. I began with an audible Bible app that read with some amount of drama and different
voices and went through the entire book of Genesis to Revelation in
about a month. (I had a lot of driving time then.) I also did a great
app for the Bible in one year by Alpha. I took in as much as I could
in large scope and also did some fine-tuning studies that dug deeper.
The clarity that came from a new understanding of how the world
works helped me make better choices, see farther ahead, avoid pit-
falls, and have less anxiety about what would be going on globally. I
had deeper peace regardless of how bad things appeared on the surface. I began to see the underlying forces at work. I found myself in
conversations with people who spoke of events and situations, but it
was as if they were talking about the will of dead leaves.

That image struck me one day as a friend was sharing a difficult
situation in her son's social circle. As she explained the circumstances,
I imagined the wind blowing around leaves in their backyard and
us looking out the window at the same scene. I imagined her saying
something like, "Look at those leaves, aren't they particularly active
today? They are flying around like crazy."

In my own mind, I would be unsure how to continue this conversation because, apparently, she had never been told about wind.
How can one explain the wind to someone who has never heard of
such a thing? My reply might be, "Well, the leaves are simply leaves.
They aren't more or less active. The wind is an invisible force that
moves the leaves around. When the wind is more active, you see the
effects with leaves appearing to move more."

We live in a time where "I'll believe it when I see it" prevails.
Yet you cannot see the wind, only the effects of it. The wind itself
is an unseen force, yet it is real and has a power to move things that
are visible. If one understands what wind is, we have a more accurate

understanding of what is happening to the leaves or random trash and objects that can be picked up and moved around, depending on the strength and power of the wind. This understanding would make us more effective at interacting with our environment. I can only imagine the confusion of these people as they see footage of a hurricane or tornado carrying off a roof or vehicle. It would create much unnecessary anxiety to think that, randomly, one's car might decide to fly into the air and crash into a building. In the least, these people may decide never to drive through Kansas. Maybe it's only cars in that state?

This is a picture of what it is like to talk to people who refuse to realize there are unseen things that are active behind the physical reality we are looking at. They tell you they are rational and scientific and only believe what they can prove. Funny, you think, they are working off of limited information and not believing in the wind is ironically unscientific. It's hard to find common language. And if someone refuses to acknowledge the wind, then you eventually learn to nod and say "uh huh." You also tend to be drawn toward people who can see the forces at work. You find yourself in much more interesting conversations about what conditions make for wind and how storms move through and if there is one coming. You can understand the physical realm better because the physical realm is generally at least one step behind the spiritual realm.

Jesus tells us plainly that there are unseen forces and a spiritual realm underpinning the physical realm we see with our human eyes. The unseen realm is as real as the things we can see and touch. But it takes spiritual eyes to see. These eyes to the unseen are often called the eyes of our heart. The greatest hope the forces of darkness have is to remain unseen to as many as possible. If they can operate under the radar, virtually invisible to humans, they have greater success disrupting, destroying, and creating division and strife among us. We end up fighting each other, not the spiritual forces that are actually creating the disruption.

> For we do not wrestle against flesh and
> blood but against the rulers, against the author-

ities, against the cosmic powers over this present
darkness, against the spiritual forces of evil in the
heavenly places. (Ephesians 6:12 ESV)

When we finally come to an understanding where the curtain
is removed, and we are able to see these forces for what they are,
it is more difficult for the forces of darkness to create chaos and
confusion. We gain the vision we need to walk in freedom, and we
bring light to the people around us. We have greater power when we
partner with God than the darkness has. Fear is vanquished, and we
can be bold as lions. We know the wind is real, and we don't have
to couch in language that makes people more comfortable. We can
plainly explain what wind is, and they can explore the concept more
or walk away.

I wrote in the previous chapter that forgiveness was my biggest
assignment in that difficult healing place. Forgiveness sounds nice.
Most people agree it is good, even necessary. What I learned is forgiveness is a bloody business. True forgiveness begins by accepting
there was a wrong committed against me and a debt (sin) created.
Some well-meaning friends tried to help me with advice like "Just
let it go" or "Don't dwell on it" or "It's the past, move on" or other
similar suggestions that were based on pretending it wasn't that big a
deal in order to not allow it to consume me. I think they considered
this the way to forgiveness. They thought forgiveness is pretending it
doesn't matter. Maybe this is the only way it can be addressed when
we don't have the power of Jesus's love behind our lives. Pretending
it's okay when someone wounds you is to hide the truth. It might
allow me to function better than being drown in the circumstances,
but this won't bring deep healing.

When a wound is covered over instead of addressed, the healing
is limited, and weakness will always be present. The wound will then
be carried forward into my future. Worse yet, it means that I cannot
be whole if someone else hurts me. This puts the power in them and
puts me subject to their actions. How can I allow myself to love and
be vulnerable and interact with boldness and care for others who
might end up hurting me? Only in the deep healing and wholeness

that comes from true forgiveness can we risk being love to a world of broken people. Broken people need love most, and they are also most likely to wound those around them. If we cannot find healing, we can't bring healing to others without fear.

Healing comes out of the truth that harm was done, and it is not okay. I would not be set free by pretending otherwise, neither would I find healing by nursing the wound, dwelling on the pain, wallowing in self-pity, and turning to a knot of bitterness. Sin is a fancy word for the destruction that comes when we hurt each other, and it is real. No matter what anyone tries to say in our modern culture, sin is alive and well. Sin is when we do harm to another, and it creates a debt against another person and ultimately against God.

Jesus came to walk the only way to freedom when we are faced with a sin debt. Make a decision to pay the debt yourself. When Jesus came, humanity had created a massive sin debt. It could never be paid off, and humanity was in deep trouble. The difference is, Jesus paid a debt we owed. When we follow his way to pay debts of others, we are not innocent. We have been forgiven much already, so we are being generous only from what has been generously given to us. The only way I have the currency to pay the debt of my neighbor is because Jesus gave it to me. He fills up the bank account, then he asks me to please spend it generously even on my enemies.

We choose to pay the debt of others because our debts have been paid already. In this season, something really wrong was done to me. However, I also knew I wasn't without fault, and I had to face squarely the part I played in the situation without any sugarcoating or excuses. Though people who loved me tried to tell me that my part "didn't deserve" the pain that came out of the situation, it didn't matter. There was power in facing head on my own darkness for what it was. It meant I could truly release it and be set free from it. When we minimize our own part in the stories we tell ourselves, we cheat ourselves from the freedom grace brings us. It helps to realize how much we have been forgiven. In fact, it seems if you could convince yourself of the depth of your need for forgiveness and the more you can find in yourself that has transgressed, the happier you are likely to be.

> I tell you her sins which are many are for-
> given—for she loved much. But he who is for-
> given little, loves little. (Luke 7:47 ESV)

In my case, I set to work learning to pay off the debt so that I could find freedom. There are four pillars I found necessary to be able to walk through this particular "death" assignment.

The first is the knowledge that I was in my own prison until the warrior prince dragged me out. I was in darkness and confusion. In that place, I created damage and sinned against other people, creating lots of debt I never paid for. It was by God's grace and love alone that I am debt-free. With that knowledge, who am I to stand in judgment against anyone else though they did hurt me? That would be to say I am better than the person who hurt me. I have been lifted out of that blindness now and am called to live differently. Having been there myself gives me more compassion for those there now.

Second is the promise that no matter how bad the wound, God assures me that He will use it for my good. He works *all things* together for the good of those who are called according to his purpose (Romans 8:28). This means I can walk forward, knowing what was intended for great destruction will be powerfully turned around in the right time to something amazing and beautiful. For this process to work, I must give it to God instead of holding on to it in bitterness or stuff it down into a box in my soul basement, pretending it didn't matter. In both cases, I'm holding on to something that God could turn into a miracle.

Third is the principle that what we sow, we also shall reap. I don't have to make someone pay for the damage they did to me, because in time, that person will find the hurt they caused me will come out of the ground in their own lives. When I understood this, it gave me more compassion on the one who hurt me. In time I saw this happen, and it gave me no pleasure when it did. Sometimes this process is used to draw others into freedom. And when we pray for our enemies, they can become fellow freedom fighters. That is exciting to see!

Last is the realization that there are spiritual forces underlying everything. The one who hurt me has become a pawn of those forces, like leaves being moved in the wind. If I rake up a leaf pile and before I can contain it, the wind rescatters it. It would be insane for me to curse the leaves. I would be behaving like a crazy person. I might curse the wind. That doesn't help much, but it's more accurate. Certainly, leaves don't make choices, and people do. So it's a limited analogy. But until someone is set free, they are only behaving the way a person in darkness can. To become a freedom fighter, one has to have an accurate understanding of who the enemy is.

In order to move forward, I must turn my training toward the forces of darkness—the true enemy. This darkness is driven by fear. Fear of loss, fear of pain, fear of rejection, fear of looking foolish. These are at the core of most ways we hurt each other (sin). The opposite of fear is love. The two things Jesus spoke most often about were love and fear.

Jesus made it clear, we must love God above all with our entire heart, soul, and strength. Then we love our neighbor as ourselves and love each other the way Jesus loved us—to the death. And if we were at all unsure, he makes it clear: Love your enemies. Pray for those who hurt you.

He also constantly told his men to fear not. He has it all in control. He was right there with them, and they were afraid. Even if it looks bad, "Don't be afraid, trust me," says the Creator of the universe. This is simple yet not easy. Love and fear are not only feelings, they are choices. We are commanded in the image of God to override the feelings of fear and choose to love—always. Why is there so much evil, pain, and suffering in the world? Because we have been given the dignity of choice. And often, we, you, I don't choose love over fear. The choice of love has a cost. If it didn't cost us something, it wouldn't really be love. The greater the cost, the greater the love, and the greater the power that flows through it. It is easy to love those who are lovely and nice to us. What makes a freedom fighter is the training and will to choose love even at great cost.

> You have heard that it was said, "You shall love your neighbor and hate your enemy." But I say to you, love your enemies and pray for those who persecute you so that you may be children of your Father in heaven. For if you love those who love you, what reward do you have? Do not even the tax collectors do the same? And if you greet only your brothers, what more do you do than others? (Matthew 5:43–44, 46–47)

The bloody business of this love and forgiveness is finding every opportunity to not extract something from the one who hurt me. It is the only way to stop the madness. I do not engage with others who speak ill of them—bonus if I can find something true and positive to say instead! I find opportunities to do something kind for them. I do not bring up the offense to them or anyone else. I do not allow my secret heart to wish their downfall or nurture thoughts of revenge even that I know I won't act out. That will rot me from the inside out. I seek these opportunities to pay out to get the debt of the wound paid sooner than later because I hate dragging this out.

I fail often. But failure is an opportunity to grow, and I do not give in to the darkness.

The more I tried these steps, the more freedom I found. The wound had less hold over me each day. Instead of being twisted up in bitterness, I was finding joy and freedom. Here is where the power of resurrection is essential. I found many moments where I failed or where I wanted to choose the better path, but it was almost impossible to get my heart to line up with what I knew was right. This is where I begged for help from the spirit that God promised to enable us to do the impossible. And when I asked for the power to overcome that darkness in my heart, I was never turned down. One step at a time, I was trying out the power entrusted to me to overcome the forces of darkness, starting with the ones in my own heart.

I was learning to become a freedom fighter.

# Chapter 6

# Operating System

Freedom fighters all run from a different operating system than the one provided at birth.

Recently I heard a doctor, Bruce Lipton, speaking on a podcast about the subconscious as a kind of hard drive that runs the program of our lives. He talked about studies that show most of these programs are set between birth to around age seven. And after that, we are running this operating system for life. The discussion was intended to give people an understanding in order to override the system and change their lives for the better. His advice was about operating from our hopes and dreams instead of the old programs. It sounded exciting, but the implementation of how to do so was unclear.

In reality, no matter what we do to update the hard drive, the operating system platform is the same. It might instill a kinder, better version of ourselves as we are enlightened about the benefits of positive thinking, intentional living, meditating, eating healthy, getting enough sleep, finding work we enjoy, becoming more productive, wasting less time, educating ourselves, learning better habits, and being present in the moment with ourselves in our environment and with those around us. This is all good. It is unquestionably preferential to the opposite: life on an operating system running unquestioned in the background, potentially not serving our lives and those around us well.

As I pondered all of this and considered my own operating system, I liked the analogy. However, I realized that I now have two hard drives. When I made the decision to follow Jesus and accept that royal adoption into his family, I was given an entirely new operating system. I have the choice every day (and throughout the day) which operating system I will run on. The old system is more familiar and comfortable, but the new system is light years more powerful and faster and runs entirely new programs that blow the old ways out of the water. It's exciting at first, but it doesn't take long to realize that there are so many layers to it that I can't imagine ever learning to use it expertly. It takes focus and energy to learn to function in it. And it takes a complete change of heart to do it. In short, it takes a miracle to switch over.

The platform of each system lies in the simple question: Who is God?

The old system we are all born into answers: I am god.

The new system concedes: God is God. I am not.

> Now we have received not the spirit of this world but the spirit who is from God that we might understand the things freely given to us by God. The natural person does not accept the things of the spirit of God, for they are folly to him, and he is not able to understand them. We have been given the mind of Christ. (1 Corinthians 2:12, 14, 16b)

The longer I live with this foundational understanding, the more aware I am of the operating systems all around me. Like *The Matrix* movie, behind the surface layer, we see with our own eyes is a computer code that generates it all—everything distilled to ones and zeros, darkness and light. When you understand the code, you can see it in action like the wind behind the leaves.

In the discussion, the doctor explained we only struggle because we are not in harmony with nature. And since we are all part of the natural world, all part of nature, we, as humans, create strife and negative environment. We poison the planet and hurt each other. For the record, the natural world isn't doing so great on its own right now either. Survival in the jungle is bloody among the food chain. And even within a species, animals can be left out in the cold to die because they don't have a pack or herd and aren't accepted. If you check the Bible for this code, we are told that:

> For the creation waits with eager, longing for the revealing of the Sons of God. For the creation was subjected to futility, not willingly, but because of him who subjected it, in hope that the creation itself will be set free from its bondage to corruption and obtain the freedom of the glory of the children of God. For we know that the whole creation has been groaning together until now. (Romans 8:19–22)

We aren't in harmony with nature. And we are told here that in fact, it *is* our fault that nature is subject to futility. It's our selfishness and determination to be god that has also put nature and creation itself on a crash course of destruction. No wonder all of creation is in hope of the revelation of the good Creator King to return, revealing the ones who have chosen love, and all of creation will be restored to perfection, and death and suffering will be banished. This thankfully includes nature and the animal kingdom!

So it is not hard to agree with Dr. Lipton that we are not in harmony with nature or the people around us in our natural old state. It is also true that we are created to be in harmony with the natural world and each other. Most of us even find we are at war with ourselves half of the time. We are not naturally in harmony with anything or anyone for long while we insist on our own way.

The fact that we want to be in harmony with nature cannot be fixed by simply trying to be in harmony with nature. Similarly, telling myself not to worry rarely makes me stop worrying, or telling myself not to be angry isn't the solution to anger issues. We need something more than knowledge to change the operating system. Many people are looking to be a better version of ourselves, but what will make a significant change is actually a new me—a new operating system.

If we operate from the original system, the best-case scenario could look like delayed gratification or deferring because it serves our future interest. That is at least a beginning. For most people, the day-to-day program will run in the background not being questioned at all. We move through the world without even realizing we are behaving and reacting as if we are god. Certainly, we rationalize—we are an intelligent, creative, benevolent god. If everyone would simply see it our way, things would be so much better. In fact, much of what we do is for someone else's own good. They just don't see it yet. At some point, when we all serve ourselves as god, we are going to come into conflict. Disharmony is inevitable.

For most, the operating system is so deeply embedded that if someone were to confront us with the notion we are playing god, we would laugh and say it is ridiculous. Yet I challenge you to look around for the evidence. It is easier to spot from the outside, so begin there. Once you begin to see it around you, if you have the fortitude, you are able to see it in your own heart as well.

Consider a few basic examples: the mother who hides the college acceptance letter to the school she doesn't think her daughter should go to; the father who is physically abusive to his son to toughen him up to survive in the world; the company who lies about environmental damage to increase the bottom line, improving the financial lives of employees and shareholders alike; the "prolife" extremist who kills an abortion doctor; the liberal-minded neighbor preaching tolerance yet hates the right-wing guy down the block; the news reporters who withholds information because it doesn't fit the story they want to tell; the husband who refuses to forgive himself for cheating on his wife even after she has forgiven him; the toddler who screams in the cereal aisle insisting on her favorite sugary breakfast.

All of these run from the operating system of "I am god" at the core. On the surface, this innocently whispers, "I know what is best."

This operating system traces all the way back to the garden story. Eve was tempted to be the one to decide good and evil, to be like God. That was the apple. God walked as a friend with them and gave them an entire world to eat, drink, and enjoy. Only one tree he asked them to leave alone. The apple itself wasn't bad. In fact, the story says the apple was good for food and a delight to the eyes. The point was there had to be one thing God requested to allow his friends to show him love in return. Love cannot exist without choice.

God told them to please eat from everything here with the exception of that one tree. Imagine the biodiversity of fruit trees that exists, and imagine that all of those except one were available to them. That gave them free will to choose love and honor the one who gave them everything else around them. The apple itself didn't bring them the shame that came immediately, the disharmony with themselves, with God, and with their environment. It was the regret that they chose self instead of love. I know what that feels like. Every day there are moments when I realize I chose the old system and did something out of fear or selfish desire, and it has the potential to hurt myself or someone else.

In order to come to peace with each other and with nature around us, we have to get in harmony with God. Once we settle the question that we are not God, that there is a God, and that we can let him run the entire universe, including our own life, he provides the operating system that allows us the power to now be in harmony with the world around us, including the environment, family, friends, those who hate us, and most importantly, ourselves. If I love my husband, and he has a request that is meaningful to him and possible for me, even if I don't understand why, I try to honor it because it shows love. This is what the apple is about. Who do you love? Will you submit to a request by the one who loves you most? Or in the end, do you always insist on your own way?

Instead of fighting God for rulership of the universe, which puts us in constant conflict with each other as we all strive for control, we submit that God is better at the job, and we hand over the keys. We are called to intentionally submit our day, our thoughts, our actions to the Creator King of the universe, the living God. This also unifies me with others who have the same system. We now are aligned with a common platform. Adam and Eve were best friends until the apple incident. Then they started the blame game, and it hurt their relationship too.

When I step down from controlling the universe, my stress and anxiety levels are significantly reduced. When I stop trying to control the people and circumstances around me, I can love with a real love, not a love that at the core is saying, "I love me. And if you enhance my life, then I love you. If you make my life difficult, then I do not love you anymore because who I really love is myself."

This means more harmony between people and better healthy relationships. The more people operating from this system, the more harmony we get. But even one person in a group can begin to influence positive change.

I want to clarify that not everyone who goes to a church or has read the Bible or calls themselves a Christian actually operates from this new platform. Going to a church does not make one a Jesus follower, and even a Jesus follower can get flipped back to the old operating system for a day, for years, or a situation. Perfection isn't promised. We have to make the choice constantly and intentionally how to live.

I've heard people say that human nature is basically good. And as long as we have the right environment, education, and opportunities, we will express our good selves. Evil, selfish behavior, is created by lack of quality in environment and is reversible by changing the circumstances. It seems obvious to me that we are born thinking we are the center of the universe. And any toddler, especially one in a fortunate environment, exhibits naturally egocentric behavior. We come into the world as little gods, and it's only the eventual heart change of submission to put the actual Creator King on the throne by choice that we can kill the selfish nature and begin to learn real love.

This is powerful to understand. God, through Jesus, offers us the ability to be unmoved and unshaken by our environmental circumstances! We cannot control where we were born, the community we grow up in, the messages of our parents, our financial background, and we have limited control over most of our environment on a good day. Yes, we make choices, but we aren't limitless in those choices. Yet Jesus explains that we can have a change inside us, inside our hearts, that means no matter what our circumstances, we can *be* love, we can *be* light, we can operate from a better place in power that doesn't come from outside in the world around us, and it doesn't exactly come from deep within either. This power comes from Him, from above us. It is also a choice, and it has a cost. To live this way costs us everything. He is willing to give us everything in exchange for everything we have to give—ourselves—and our god illusion of control. In truth, it's like giving up toothpicks and popsicle sticks and being given a castle. Yet have you ever tried this with a two-year old? Whatever they have at the time is "mine," and they can't quite make the logical leap yet to hand over the popsicle stick for a bike, a car, or a house. They don't even understand yet what that is. We do this all the time.

This is an unpopular message I know. We all want to look in the mirror and see the inherently good person we know is in there. But do we truly know our own hearts? The ancient writings of Jeremiah of ancient Israel tells us we don't.

> The heart is deceitful above all things
> and desperately sick; who can understand it?
> (Jeremiah 17:9 ESV)

No one wants to face that this is true of the person in the mirror. How else could so much wrong have been done over the history of the world by people certain they were doing the right thing or following their hearts? Wars, crusades, genocide, mutilation—these are only the worst of them. None of us want to face that our hearts can lie to us, taking us to places we should run from. A reason many people cannot imagine making the switch to running on God's operating system is not being able to see that we are actually unfit to be god of our own lives or anyone else's. The truth of this switch is frightening: "You mean, give up what I want? Give up my entire platform for some other way of living where I have to do things I may not want to do?" It sounds absurd, especially if you haven't come to realize your heart can lie to you.

It is the upside-down way—give up your life to find life, lay it down in order to pick it up. It seems all wrong, backward. It's a huge leap. It's risky. It's not for the faint of heart. In fact, my guess as to why most people must come to the end of themselves entirely to try it is because when there is nothing else that is working, your operating system keeps crashing the program. And you finally see you are working on a flawed machine and are never going to get where you had hoped. You just might be ready to take a risk for something new.

When I agreed to make the switch, and I did it gradually but intentionally, one program at a time to see if it worked. I asked the living God of the universe to take over, and it was powerful. I now had an elegantly designed platform that worked with tech support that is out of this world. In time I realized how wonderful this promise truly was:

Delight yourself in Adonai, and he will give
you your heart's desire. (Psalm 37:4 CJV)

This operating system has one entry point: Love Adonai, the Lord, with all your heart and all your soul and with all your mind. That's the password. It's completely inclusive, available to anyone. And the cost is the same no matter who you are: everything.

Contrary to the lies that keep people on a constant path of failure, you don't live a good life to get it. You don't clean yourself up and then come to God with something he might find valuable that you've accumulated. You only have to realize your operating system is broken and limited, and it doesn't make a difference if it's still on the original platform from your broken childhood or been upgraded dutifully each year. You realize no matter how good or terrible you are, you are still completely inept at being god, and you are ready to give it up. It's a hard addiction to break. In fact, as long as we live here, we struggle with it. But if we ask, we will always be granted to power to overcome ourselves. Even so, we are never forced. This is why there is evil and pain in the world by that way. But that is an entirely different chapter. God doesn't force his operating system on anyone.

The crazy, wonderful truth is that when we take a sledgehammer to the old hard drive and kill our platform of destructive living for ourselves, we begin to break free and are granted an entirely new life. We see the truth that this verse isn't only in the call to delight ourselves in God in a great romance (which is in itself quite amazing), but he promises to give us our heart's desire. And the upside-down reality of that is we are finally able to see that we didn't even know our own hearts before. We only thought we did.

How often have you watched someone invest much or all of their resources into something they were certain would fulfill them, and then get it only to find it left them empty. Often this cost them everything—their family, their health, their lives—and they stand there in a terrifying moment, realizing that the thing they thought was the desire of their heart was not apparently actually the thing. Some of these people commit suicide. Others jump into the next venture, the next extreme adventure, the next relationship, doubling down in the hope that more or different will satisfy with much of the cost passed on to the world around them.

Some never achieve the thing. Some risk it all for something they never find. The chase consumes their life. Some people are satisfied for a time, yet nothing is stable on this earth. Death, financial crashes, illness, disaster take away the thing they had found stability and enjoyment in, leaving the person in grief and loss. Then there is the life afraid to hope, the life lived small and safe, dreams and desires locked in a box to suffocate over time. The risk of disappointment is too great.

One thing all those who are able to switch over to the new operating system share is the surprise of stumbling into the amazing gifts that Adonai, the beloved, set out for his lovers. The expression of surprise is two-fold. Wow! I had no idea I wanted this. And how did you know? To find the things that most satisfy me are sometimes a surprise at first and then bring abundance of joy and peace. Even more importantly, they are gifts. The promise isn't that if you work really hard, you can earn the desires of your heart. It is so much better than that. The promise reads: Love Adonai, delight in him, and he will *give* you the desires of your heart. They are bestowed, given, dropped into your life. This is the opposite of the world's system.

All this takes time and patience. God's time is rarely easy for me to rest in. It takes great patience, perseverance, and a lot of trust. I have watched God weave together things expertly as only he is able, situations I submitted to his authority even when it made zero sense to me and seemed unreasonably painful. I often thought if I only switched back to my own system for a short time, I could probably do better with this particular thing. Thankfully, the whisper always reminds me gently that my track record isn't very good on my own, so I might as well sit it out.

Even in a short time, I have been blown away by the glorious tapestry he's woven together from the fragments I gave him to work with. In my own platform, I had a little split-level house in mind, a big yard maybe, but he made a big mess of the toothpicks and popsicle sticks I'd assembled so carefully. And while I camped out in the yard, over time I could see the makings of a castle emerge. He grins deviously when I begin to see the outline of a new tower. Castles take much longer to erect. But in my heart runs the blood of a queen, so I wait.

# Chapter 7

# Daughter of the King

In the midst of my years of struggle, I came across Bob Goff's books. In the book *Love Does*, he asks the questions *Who are you?* and *Who are you becoming?*

These questions are of utmost importance and will change the entire trajectory of your life as you take them on with intention.

Throughout time, there are specific instances when the angel of the Lord (the malakh YHWH) came to earth and interacted directly with a human. The malakh YHWH is no ordinary angel. It is said this description is saved for the pre-incarnated Jesus, God himself, appearing in a way that a human could understand and interact with. My attention was brought to the curious fact that when the situation was so important that God didn't send a messenger but decided the message was so vital he was going to handle it himself. The message was often one of identity.

Someone needed to be told or reminded *who* they were.

Our identity determines how we move through this world. When I came to see the truth that my daddy is the only living God and Creator King of the universe, it changed everything.

If you came to see right now that you had royal blood and were part of a royal family of the very kingdom of heaven, how would it change your day?

What does it mean to be royalty of an eternal kingdom?

I want to take back the cultural context of the word *princess*. If you look in the urban dictionary, some of the definitions of princess read: a girl that has been pampered, sheltered, and spoiled all her life to the extent that she has no idea about the real world. She may be used to getting what she wants but only because she deserves the absolute best, admired by many but is too good of a girl for anyone / She can be spoiled at times.

A friend had teased me after hiking a mountain trail together that, apparently, I wasn't only a princess who needed to be carried around on a horse. As I considered my response, I said I do enjoy riding my horses, and, indeed, I am a princess but that I don't think that means what you think it means. My friend got serious for a moment and wanted to be sure I didn't take offense to the remark. Calling someone a princess carries the implication that one is out of touch with reality, spoiled, and probably fragile. That is when I decided in my own life, and those of the women around me, we must retake the cultural context of princess.

When I consider myself a daughter of the Creator King, his princess child, I consider that it is not about how I expect to be treated but how I will interact with the world. Once again, it is not about reacting to my circumstances but the new operating system I draw from within. I will live a life of honor and grace. I will treat those around me with dignity because of my identity not because of their actions. I will choose to be patient and kind even when it's hard. I will choose to be generous with my resources even if I have little to give. I will support and champion others in their worthy dreams and goals and be glad when the ones I care about succeed. I won't be afraid to get my hands dirty in the tasks I'm called to but will also take the time to "clean up" and dress in elegance and beauty when the time is right. My elegance will come from a place of knowing my worth and not needing to be sexually alluring on the surface to have value. I will be bold and courageous to speak when I need to and be quiet and will listen when I am called to. I will chase humility and meekness even when they are hard to grasp. I will use my head as well as my heart.

I recommend the story of *A Little Princess* by Frances Hodgson Burnett. She tells a beautiful story of Sara, a young girl who went from riches to rags then back to riches and kept the heart of a princess in both plenty and in want. She was a princess to those around her even when she suffered. Here is one of my favorite quotes:

> "If I *was* a princess—a *real* princess," she murmured, "I could scatter largess to the populace. But even if I am only a pretend princess, I can invent little things to do for people. Things like this." She was just as happy as if it was largess. "I'll pretend that to do things people like is scattering largess. I've scattered largess."

Sara decided that her identity could be one of a princess's regardless of her external circumstances. She knew who she was and walked through her days as an heiress with the finest dresses or as a scullery maid with little to eat and no heat in her room, determined to find good things to do for others. I have come to believe that the biggest problem we face today is the loss of our identity. It's difficult enough to remember who we are on our own in this broken world, but the lies ravaging about us every day about women tear us apart at every turn.

When we lose the truth of who we were created to be, we act like lost souls hurting ourselves and others. We behave without honor in both rags and riches alike. Even those in great wealth can act like paupers of the heart in how they treat the people around them. It is from the heart, not from the bank account, that we see the true nature.

> The good person out of the good treasure of his heart produces good, and the evil person out of his evil treasure produces evil, for out of the abundance of the heart his mouth speaks. (Luke 6:45 ESV)

Don't you see that nothing that enters a person from the outside can defile them? For it doesn't go into their heart but into their stomach and then out of the body. He went on: 'What comes out of a person is what defiles them. For it is from within, out of a person's heart, that evil thoughts come."

There are places in the world where girls are not allowed to be educated and treated as less than the boys in the culture. This is a lie of darkness that valiant men and women fight against each day. I am inspired at how Bob Goff has risked his life opening schools in war zone areas and places with dark regimes to open schools that accept girls and orphans. It would appear that few things are more dangerous to oppressive regimes than championing and educating their girls!

In many of these cultures, women are also required to cover their entire bodies head to foot with only their eyes uncovered so they can see where they are going. The cultural mandate to hide a woman completely sends the message that men cannot be responsible for controlling how they see a woman. The sight of her is too powerful. These regimes want to control their population to the extent that women are not even able to be seen. Men should not or cannot be trusted to control their minds when faced with a beautiful woman. If you are reading this with a western cultural viewpoint, this is obviously oppressive and extreme. Yet there is also danger on the opposite end, and that may be where the western cultural viewpoint leaves a blind spot.

Girls learn quickly that they have power in beauty and sexuality and even at young ages begin to wield this power like a weapon. There are many studies that tell us what we instinctively know: Attractive women get farther in our society than those who aren't born with what we see today as beautiful features. Attractive women who learn how to use their beauty and sexuality as a tool are often highly successful.

All the same, we also see women unable to occupy many places successfully as men do. This is a challenging area to delve into with many broken layers. In some cases, it is a simple oppressive force that devalues what a woman offers because she is not a man. This is always wrong. Yet there are fields and jobs that women are frankly not as well suited as men are. This doesn't mean they cannot do them, and not all women have the same interests or strengths. I cannot solve the deeper broken layers of this issue here. Something I will press into is that we know that in God's eyes, women are loved and valued equally to men. Jesus often showed a special honor toward women. Yet what about the western culture message of feminism? Does it do women a service to say we should be the same as men? It sounds good, equal rights. God did give us equal human rights as he created man and woman in his own image. However, he called Eve *ezer kenegdo*. I love this. It is weakly translated as helpmate or helper in many English Bibles. But the meaning has so much more depth and power.

*Ezer kenegdo* is powerful help, strength, opposite of man. We all as humanity share in God's image in our uniqueness. None of us have enough of the image for a complete picture. Each person created has a unique place to fill in the great story of the world. But on a broader level, man and woman have different, equally important characteristics of God's character. And within those characteristics are levels of shading and strength and, due to sin, weakness as well. Why bother creating man and woman if they were to be the same? That is a lie that takes the dark oppression of women and swings the pendulum to the other extreme. The message to fix the oppression is that we should equate men and women. This damages women's unique characteristics and takes away from the *ezer kenegdo* role she was given as the crowning jewel of creation. They both are lies from the pits of hell.

Notice the entire universe, world, garden, and man were all in place before God introduced Eve to the scene. There is something beautiful and special about that honor. As far as I understand, she was the final crowning moment of creation. And in the words *ezer kenegdo*, she was given a special place in it. This doesn't make women better than men either. Men were intended to be our champions. Sadly, the real identity of men is also broken, and dark forces have made deep inroads to destroying the honor, power, and courage men were created to carry through life. When our strengths get twisted and misused, women wield sexuality as a tool, and men use their strength to abuse and control.

When men and women rediscover the redeemed nature of these roles and live into their unique qualities and gifts, it is a beautiful picture. As I spent time with God in healing from a difficult divorce, I did not decide never to love again, nor did I want to rush into another unbalanced relationship. In the depths of my heart, I began to see that if I was a daughter of the King. What I needed was a prince worthy of my heart, not a perfect man because we are still here on broken earth, and I am not a perfect woman. Still the great romance that God created between himself and us is played out here even imperfectly for now.

I began to ask God if he wanted me to have another love in this life. Would he give me the patience to wait for the prince who was chosen for me by the King and was worthy of my heart, I asked that he would come to win my love with the dragon head in hand. As the age-old song cries, "I need a hero! I'm holding out for a hero till the end of the night." And instead of doing it the accepted western cultural way I had before, I wanted to try to do it differently. Instead of going out there to get the guy I thought I wanted in my life, instead of using the way I dressed or talked to lure in a man I thought was going to be great, I decided to put all my chips into the reality I said I believed: God is real, He's personal, and He has a plan. So unless I heard otherwise, I was going to wait in the castle for someone who would pursue the heart of the favored daughter of the King.

Does that sound like a fairy tale? Do you hear your heart telling you it's ridiculous? Is the voice from inside telling you to grow up and get with the real world? This isn't how it happens.

My friend, those are the lies that bind our hearts. There is a reason we love those stories. There is a reason that little girls love the Disney princesses—from Snow White to Mulan. Before we were ruined by the dark forces that have taken this world hostage, we knew that we were created for this story. We know that we are worthy of a great prince who will do something of courage and honor to get our attention. If this strikes a nerve, take a quiet moment to dig deeper here and explore the tug in your heart for this romance. It is not that we seek a courageous prince because we are weak. No! It is because we begin to see who we are and how valued our hearts are. In fact, the courageous prince might have valor and strength, but he is incomplete without an *ezer kenegdo*, a worthy beloved that brings balance and opposite strength to the whole.

Regardless if you are married to a prince or not, and regardless if you are single and have never fallen in love—and especially if you are in a relationship—you are cultivating. This story is true. C. S. Lewis has insightful explanations of why we are drawn to romance, beauty, and all good things here. They are but a thin shadow of the thing we are truly made for. The true great romance of our hearts is that God is that hero. He is the beloved. And depending on where you are, he could be outside the prison door with sweat, blood, and tears trying at all costs to rescue you from the dark place; or he could be the warrior outside the castle tower standing triumphantly with the dragon head, asking the King for your hand because he knows you are made for him. So regardless of your circumstances here and now, until you see the real great romance God is writing for you as his beloved, you will struggle to find health and balance in the earthly romances you enter into.

I had begun this process of healing while married to a man I believed could be restored into a prince but was struggling with battles of his own. I know God has the power to restore. He brings dead men to life. Yet in this case, it was not his way to do so, at least not in the time that I had hoped. He had different plans for both of our lives.

After many months of quiet and intense healing, I came to understand the real warrior of my heart was Yeshua (Jesus), the one who wrote himself into the story to find me about two thousand years back. When my human husband moved out, Yeshua moved in. It was a presence that was strong and almost palpable. Through the darkest times, I grieved. But oddly enough, I never felt alone and wasn't lonely either. He was here. Those who have experienced this mystery know how real it is. Those who haven't yet might struggle understanding. It was him, and him alone, that walked my heart through the layers it took to make me whole, like an intense year of therapy without a bill.

I came to know that I would love to share my life with someone but that my adventures with Yeshua would never leave me bored or lonely, and that truly would be what would best satisfy my soul. Some women are only for him. As crazy as that sounds to some, it is a reality for others. I gave that determination to his capable hands and settled into my castle. Adonai is the one who knows the true desire of my heart and what I was created for. I would allow him to reveal even this in his time. I live in a rural county with not one stoplight, mostly national forest land, more cows than humans, and I spend my days teaching or in the solitary forests on my horses. If my prince would come, he was going to need a good map to find me.

Instead of desperately running into a new relationship, I dug into my identity and learned what it meant to be a woman in God's eyes. Jesus chose women to be the first witnesses to his resurrection from the dead. He chose a woman to be the one he revealed the truth of who he was to the world at the Samaritan well. God has a special place for women, and his princesses are cared for, protected, and have deep strength running through them—the kind of strength that when called to do so can save a nation by running a tent peg through the temple of an evil general. It is no accident a woman was chosen for that role. The general sensed no threat from a simple housewife. Jael was uniquely qualified to serve her nation that day because of the lie of darkness that women are not a force to be concerned with.

If the messages I'd been programmed with from my youth— that my value and power rest in my appearance or sexuality, or that I am the same as any man—is not the truth, then what is?

My value and identity came from being chosen by God the King. I wasn't even simply born into this family, I was pursued, brought in, adopted, betrothed, wanted. The King sent the crown prince to get me out of that dark prison at any cost and bring me home because of who I am. My appearance and sexual draw will fade over time, but the unique things that make me who I am will never fade. I was created for a purpose here that no one else can fill. Instead of trying to go through life as my own god, deciding what is good and bad for me, what I want to get, and who I want to be, now my life became about asking the one who made me these questions: Who am I? What am I here to do? What will make me the most fulfilled in this life? Who have you chosen to partner with me in the journey? What parts of my personality are beautiful that you want to develop, and what parts do you want me to let go of because they don't serve me or anyone else?

This search is about me. But it's about how the one who made me sees me. It's about giving up insisting I know best, and instead becoming curious to find out my true purpose. If we all showed up as a cosmic accident and have no purpose, and life is short, and then you die—the end—why bother making hard choices to love other people or to sacrifice to serve? Nothing matters anyway. Yet most people, even who don't know God, still say there is value in love and service. They can't say why. I once heard Tim Keller refer to this as intellectual schizophrenia. It doesn't actually fit logically into their worldview, yet don't we still somehow know? There is a seed in all of us that knows we are created for more than a cosmic accident to just be happy, if possible, in a small comfortable life.

When you find out who you were created to be you when you step into your identity, you don't have to be the most alluring woman in the room. You don't have to wield your beauty like a weapon. You don't have to dress in a way to draw attention and show your power. And you do not have to hide either. A true princess doesn't have to wield force everywhere she goes to be sure she is noticed. When you are royalty, nothing can take that away from you. And you can walk comfortably through life with grace and treat others with humility because you didn't choose and earn your rank in the first place. You begin to live gratefully instead of entitled. You don't have to work the room because everything already belongs to your Father. And you will always have everything you need when you need it and nothing more than you need, so you don't have to carry it. On the other end, you do not have to hide. You are fully known and fully loved no matter what has happened to you in your past and what you've done. When the crown prince carries you out and covers you in his cloak, you are royalty now. And he pays the old debts so you can begin clean.

As a royal woman, I do want to take care of my appearance. Beauty is a gift from the Creator, and I don't discount the value of it. We should celebrate beauty in all its forms from a creative mind to symmetrical delicate features, great fashion sense, or a fabulous head of hair. It is a matter of the heart when women go from taking care of their body and dressing well to wielding their appearance or sexuality like a weapon.

When you are pulled out of the prison of darkness and set in the castle, once you see the love lavished on you to make you his own daughter, once your heart has gone through that healing, you begin to see who you are, and you can begin to walk through the world with a heart that flows living water and grace everywhere you go. Regardless of how you are treated and no matter what physical things you possess, even if you have nothing, you will still find ways to do kind things for people. That is the heart of a princess.

# Chapter 8

# Choose This Day

But if serving the Lord seems undesirable to you, then
choose for yourselves this day whom you will serve, whether
the gods your ancestors served beyond the rivers or the
gods of the Amorites in whose land you are living. But
as for me and my household, we will serve the Lord.

—Joshua 24:15 ESV

There is a war for this world and the people here. The more my eyes adjust to the light, the clearer it becomes. There are forces of darkness that come against joy, healing, and goodness. Those who say there is no evil are in denial, blinded, or lying. Evil is most definitely real. Genocide, human trafficking, child abuse, governmental corruption, systematic injustice are all evidence of real evil alive today. Evil must be opposed, or it will grow and consume until all is lost. That is the nature of evil: destruction, complete destruction. Evil is so bent on destruction that its ultimate goal is to destroy everything, including its own agency in the end. This is why evil's best trick is to convince us it's not real. You won't invest time opposing something you don't believe exists.

This is good news. Many people who don't want to acknowledge the truth of evil prefer a less offensive story. They want to hope that if evil doesn't exist then maybe the right social program or access to education will bring about a better world, that we will evolve. Yet they miss the best story of all when they insist on trying to cram this square peg reality into some alternate round hole paradigm. The existence of evil necessitates the existence of opposite evil—goodness, love, mercy, justice, truth, sacrifice, service, patience, kindness. These are all evidence that there is also a force of good active in the world. If there is no evil, then we cannot rationally believe in goodness. If we then accept there are two opposing forces active in the world, that is a war.

The war of good and evil is alive and well today, and we are all involved. I realize many of us wish we could stay neutral; that isn't a real option. A favorite quote of mine is "The greatest trick the devil played on mankind is that he doesn't exist." It's been attributed to enough people. I'm not sure who to accurately quote. But it is a basic truth. I can understand why people would like to make up an alternate reality to avoid dealing with evil. Evil is powerful and terrible and, when faced directly, can be downright frightening. It's easier to do a peace treaty and go on about your day. I mean, what chance do you, small weak humans, have against the forces of hell anyway? No chance—not on our own anyway. It's true. If you're not ready to choose the protection of the one who can protect you, you might as well make a treaty with the darkness and try to have a nice little life here for now. In case you aren't sure how a treaty works, it puts you in an agreement with darkness. You say, "I won't bother you if you don't bother me." This means, in order to put your head down and have a happy little life, you aren't neutral, you are in agreement with the dark side. You are now on the side of the evil one. However, I said there is good news, and the story is so much better because there is another option.

Choose to align with the true King.

This is the mighty one, the only God who is living and powerful and active from the beginning of time and today and will be ongoing into the future of how this war plays out/ And it will continue to play out until it ends. It will end. All things here on this broken earth end. We see this everywhere around us. This world *is* finite. But we were created for more. And so we hunger for the better story, the one where good prevails, and justice is served. And mercy is offered to those who seek it. And all things are made right when the good King returns. Why does happily ever after sell so well especially to children who haven't been ravaged by the war yet? Because we are created for the garden. We are created for happily ever after. My friend, it is all true. And even if we weren't told the end of the story, wouldn't you rather die bringing good to the world around you than live comfortably being part of the spread of darkness? Freedom is having something worth dying for because then you truly begin to live!

What would happen if you allowed your heart to entertain the idea that there is a great romance, to sit in the truth that there is a beloved who will go through death and hell to win your heart? There is an album by Christy Nockels, *Be Held; Lullabies for the Beloved*, that impacted me in a difficult season. And one song in particular illustrates this in a tender and beautiful way:

Always Remember to Never Forget

Hey there, beautiful one, you there shining with glory
Would you let your heart hear if I sang about you
Did you know that every fairy tale you love
They have borrowed your story
Of a maiden so lovely and a hero so true

It's just that this world is hollow
And it wants to swallow
Any memory of who you really are

Like a treasure in the deep, your heart is a diamond
And your hero will do what it takes to find it
So he can hold it tenderly and become your defender
He even lay down His life just to make your heart heal

It's just that this world is broken
And it wants to hold back
Any evidence of that kind of love

So always remember to never forget
When you look in the mirror, the answer is yes
Yes, you are pure as gold. Yes, you are beautiful
So always remember to never forget
Always remember to never forget

This world is hollow and broken. And the war for your heart is to shut it down, starve it of goodness, and steal your hope. If you live in fear, you will have at least little impact for good or possibly be a tool for destruction. This happens to most of us in some degree as we grow up and are disappointed. People in our lives who have made truces with darkness in hope of protecting themselves and those they love inadvertently damage our innocence and our hopes. Then there are those who have embraced evil, and they do deeper damage to children as they grow up in abusive situations who beg and pray and do not find the rescue they seek. It is real, and it is heartbreaking. The prince of evil does not fight fair. No innocence is out of his target zone, and this is a reason some understandably rail against the concept of a true God and King who is good. How could He allow that to go on?

Yet I've never seen anyone ask the question: If there is a God who is good, how can he allow me to continue to disappoint and cause pain in the world around me day-to-day? How can he allow me to live in this truce with the darkness, looking the other way so we can all get along? And yet we all do this at least from time to time. It is much easier for us to justify and rationalize the way we hurt those around us that never seems as bad as what we see in others. I cannot answer all the questions of the broken hearts that read these lines. And it isn't my intent to write that book right now. Still I do know this: God has promised to make everything right. I cannot imagine what it would look like for God to take some of the most horrific situations evil brings through mankind and make it *right*. Restoration and redemption are his greatest joy. And I know that the joy that will come when the tables are turned—and it is all finally dealt with—will be richer and more powerful in relation to darkness that brought the pain to begin with.

I came to understand the impact of this message through listening to Tim Keller. One of his favorites quotes from J. R. R. Tolkien in the Lord of the Rings trilogy when Sam Gamgee sees his great friend alive after he had seen him fall to his death many chapters and adventures before. Sam had hoped to stay neutral but was called into the war of good and evil and is one of the greatest friends and unsung heroes of literature!

> Gandalf! I thought you were dead! But then I thought I was dead myself. Is everything sad going to come untrue? What's happened to the world?
>
> A great Shadow has departed," said Gandalf, and then he laughed, and the sound was like music or like water in a parched land. And as he listened, the thought came to Sam that he had not heard laughter, the pure sound of merriment, for days upon days without count.

God tells us, so we won't be confused by how things appear here in the physical world that he has allowed a time for evil to have its way with those who choose it on this earth. We live in that time. But the time will end. And when the great shadow is removed, something along the lines of everything sad becoming untrue awaits us.

Each person makes a choice. Even in not choosing, we choose to: embrace evil because it promises short term gain (greed, pleasure, entertainment, fame), make a truce with evil because it promises false peace for this present time, or resist evil and join forces with the one who someday *will* make everything right. As image bearers, God gives us the dignity of choice and causation. Our choices have impact. That is a great power and responsibility. The stakes are real and so are the consequences humans often choose poorly and cause much pain and destruction.

I have chosen, at different stages in my life, all three approaches. I have tried to make a truce and live a happy life in my own little corner. I thought I could make a nice balance of God as a safety net along with the day-to-day of living what I thought was reasonably good enough. It doesn't work. This is called being double-minded, and over time, if you don't completely kill off your deeper soul and spirit (the kernel of truth we are made with), it will eventually drive you a little crazy. After the life I had created in my best efforts imploded brilliantly, I decided to give up and go all out to live for myself. If my effort to "be basically good" and fitting in to most of the world I saw around me didn't work, why bother? So I went with whatever I thought would bring me entertainment and pleasure. I made a big move to a small rural community I'd fallen in love with and felt a draw to. I can look back today and acknowledge the truth. I was aware, though I tried to ignore. I knew the place I ran to had a draw of darkness. This tiny little niggle of a knowledge I could easily push down as ridiculous. The promise of a new life that I could do whatever I wanted recreate myself in any way I chose. That was true freedom. I would find whatever my heart desired. And since I had recently blown up my "good" life that turned out to be a wreck, I was going to throw it all to the wind and chase whatever I wanted. And I did.

At first it was such fun. I did whatever I wanted and got it with any means I had at my disposal. I lived entirely for myself. I had lots of friends and spent many hours with them. In my case, God allowed me to pull the cord pretty far. He never let me go. But I wandered into many fruitless and even dangerous off roads in my own pursuits, and he waited. I was never at peace. But because I was starting over, I kept imagining that what I wanted was close, I was sure of it. If I kept going, surely around the next bend, it would be great. What I desperately wanted more than I understood was to be known and loved. I thought I could extract that from the man I was with, a man who was as broken as I was in his own heart and struggled to know and love himself. So the chances that man, without great healing, could ever know and love me were zero. Yet I am incredibly stubborn and was certain I could force it into place. If I could only draw him in deeper with whatever means I had at hand, then someday he would see me. And then he would love me, and we would finally be happy. How strange this deluded thinking that I kept pushing deeper into.

I would be whoever I thought he would be attracted to in the hopes that someday he would actually love and accept me for who I really was while also knowing that who I really was probably shouldn't be uncovered. Because when you actively pursue darkness, a deep sense of shame and being an imposter accompany. How could a man who didn't know himself ever get to know me when I was hiding out of my own shame? And how could anyone accept me when I knew that down deep, I wasn't acceptable? Oh, the heartbreak.

In trying to live this out, I can see how I both tried to wield what could make me attractive and yet still try to hide in shame. It creates an outer facade that is intended to draw and attract. But underneath that shell is emptiness and shame. I had no understanding of this at the time. Someone with greater heart vision looking in would certainly see that implosion this would eventually cause. My husband, at the time, once asked a viable question: What did you think would happen? He was directly talking about the fact as he saw it that he didn't love me and held me in unforgiveness for some things that hurt him. But in looking back, I ask myself this question of the hollow shell I had created that I wanted so much for love to enter in from outside of myself to fill it. This broken human could never accomplish that! Only the perfect love of Yeshua, sent by the very God of love, could fill that empty shell. My limited understanding didn't even consider that at first.

God never allowed me to have what I desperately sought. I have great endurance (which he will use for good), and I would have never given up and died trying. My marriage was a storm—first quietly hidden in deep layers, then it grew and worked itself closer to the surface until it was a hurricane that couldn't be ignored. It came to the point that almost any conversation would draw destructive force winds, and I found myself taking cover wondering if it would eventually pass. Like in the story of Jonah, I believe God, in his mercy, gave my husband enough seasickness to throw me out of the boat so to speak. Like the men on the ship to Tarshish, he did this to save himself. However, God had set it all up. And though it seemed like certain death, there is love under those waves. God sent a great fish to put me into time-out. Sitting in the belly of a whale, I had few options. My future was completely out of my control. I could die or heal. I actually hoped it might be death because I felt too far gone to imagine healing. Also, the inner guts of a fish are not immediately inspiring for a case to live and heal! But not one to actively kill myself, God decided for me to live. Finally, at the end of my desperation, I was ready to go all in with the one who created me. If only he would take my tangled mess of a life and sort it out into something worth living, then I would live for him because I'd finally learned that control was an illusion, and I was unfit to run my own life. I wanted to see if God could—would—come out of the trunk, take over the driving, and get me somewhere—anywhere—better than this.

I hope, dear reader, you hear one clear thread in this entire story. My healing and new life did not come because I did it all right. I did not do the things that earned me a life of restoration or a beautiful garden. I do not deserve the beautiful gifts of love lavished on me. Left on my own, I would have given up and chosen death more than once. When my first attempt at a double-minded life blew up, I did not run immediately to God's door and ask for help. On the contrary, I went all in for doing it my way and running away from God first. Just like Jonah, I had to be thrown overboard by the heathen sailors before God sent a fish to hold me from running any farther. I am not the story of how to do everything right so God can smile down on his good daughter and work on the real problems of the world. No, I am the lost one who kept running into walls and over cliffs that he never gave up on waiting for me to exhaust myself mentally and emotionally until I was ready to die. And then as I was quiet and beyond hope, he came.

Most stories I hear, though the details differ, share this grace as a common thread. Maybe not everyone has to come to the end of their own devices in order to turn to God completely, but I've heard enough to see that many do. We are the stubborn ones who keep insisting, "I can do it myself!" Like a toddler who wants to make breakfast for the family, it's going to be a disaster until Dad or Mom takes over. Then a good parent will give the toddler an important job, like stirring the pancake batter, and voila, a beautiful breakfast appears and the kitchen doesn't have to look like the aftermath of

World War IV. The good news is that God will turn that stubbornness and strong will into a strength that he pours into for good if we will let him. We do have the choice. Traumatic events will not leave you in the same place, but they have the capacity for bitterness and destruction or beauty and redemption—we decide which. The path to redemption is always harder to begin but gets easier along the way as light breaks through. And healing—always painful at first—brings strength and new life.

In dark times, I had voices and words that pierced the deep truths I could not deny: You are selfish; you are hard on people around you; you are rigid and don't care how your choices affect the world; you are driven and run over those in your path; you leave a wake of destruction wherever you go; you can be reckless and dangerous; you are too much; you are not enough. Women who loved me saw this breakdown and tried to assure me: It is not true! You are not those things.

But I was those things. That was why I had the shame and emptiness under the shell. They encouraged me, and I love them for it. I had to face the terrible truth head on and combat the lies with the identity of who I was created to be would pull them up one at a time and destroy their power over me forever. This was the path to redemption. I needed a hero! I had to take all those accusations and face them with my defender. The crowned prince is also my defense attorney. If you want a good defense, you have to be honest with your attorney. This one also happened to love me enough to assure me: If you will give it all to me—the darkest most horrible things—I will take care of them myself, and we go before the judge and begin clean. The only way forward is to plead "guilty" and hear the sentence, then my defender is also the one who goes to the court to pay all the fines I could never pay. And we walk out of the courtroom free together.

Going forward, when those voices of accusation return, I can face them directly and say, "That was who I used to be! I have been redeemed, and you've got nothing on me now! I live in freedom. Go bother someone else!" Yes, it is hard to look directly in the mirror and accept the dark things in our hearts. But the only other option is to ignore or downplay them. Someday justice will catch up. Will you be your own defense? Will the fact that someone else is actually worse than you excuse the darkness you carry? I've never seen a court work that way. Will you blame someone else or how you were raised or treated or wounded? Will you point to your circumstances? Will you rationalize your truce with the evil one because you only wanted to protect your family? In the end, we stand before the judge alone or with Yeshua. We have no excuse for ourselves that will stand up in a court of eternal justice. I know who I want defending me.

Still so many people insist on being their own defense even if they have nothing to work with. We hear that voice inside from our own deceitful hearts that says: Look around you, you are better than the person who (fill in the blank with the person you know who has done something you consider worse that whatever it is you're headed to court for). Imagine being in court for a speeding ticket. You were going ten miles per hour over the speed limit. If you happen to know the defendant in front of you was going thirty miles per hour over the limit in your ignorance of justice, you may inform the judge that you should not be penalized because your infraction is comparatively smaller than the man who was just sentenced. In no world does that defense have weight.

The enemy of our souls prefers to use truth against us, but it is always a limited and fractured truth. Darkness first draws you into the offense, then shames and convicts you when you are drawn in. The weapon against that is a greater truth. There must be justice. We know this deeply. When innocence is sinned against, our hearts cry out for justice (as long as it is for someone else). When we are standing before the judge, we have reasons for our offenses. Truly there must be justice. And God must be a God of justice if he is also to be a God of love. The difference when you call in Yeshua as your defense is that the judge takes your guilty plea, files it with the court. But before you can be hauled off to serve your sentence, the judge walks back to the desk and pays your fine in full. The debt still must be paid. The difference is who pays. Many people realize they carry guilt. Darkness turns the guilt message to shame. And sadly, they insist on paying the fine themselves. They don't want to be indebted to anyone, especially God. Yet they do not have the resources to cover the penalty they've accrued and the languish, possibly for eternity, in prison. That is the pride we carry: I will do it myself.

I don't have the resources to make right what I've done wrong. I will certainly take the offer of life and, once given that gift of life and freedom, would gladly spend the rest of my life trying to help others know they have the same choice available to them. That is a life that threatens the darkness. When the dead ends closed around me, and I sat in the fish, I finally chose this way.

The crowned prince of the Creator King looked at me in the belly of the fish. I was covered in slime and ready to die in my selfishness and self-pity. Yet he had love and compassion in his eyes for me and said: You are mine.

With passion he continued: I gave my life to have yours because of love. I know you. I know everything about you. I made you. Nothing in you is hidden from me, and I choose you. I know your debt, and I will pay off every part. I gave everything to have you. Take my hand, beloved, and be mine as I am yours. Give me everything. Let me love you.

This is what it is to be fully known and fully loved.

> WHISPER. On your own, you have been hard, selfish, and driven. You are living for things that will never satisfy and leaving destruction in your search. Let my love for you break your hard heart, and my light will pour through it like beautiful stained glass! I will raise you into someone even bigger than you were. But it will be in love and not destruction! You are more than enough when you are in me, and I'm in you! I will pay the price to set you free. You are worth it to me. You are everything.

My heart gasped and choked out seawater as it began to come alive. I knew it. The thing I had always tried to find was being offered, and it meant life and freedom. This offer of freedom, I would be insane to refuse: Choose this day. Choose my love, and you will never be empty again. Dance with me in the storms that come, and you will have peace. Learn who I see in you, and destroy the weapons of darkness against you. Stand up, take my hand, and let's *go*.

# Chapter 9

# The Greatest Love of All

O nce we choose this love and begin to walk in it, that love pours through us. We begin to look strange to the rest of the world. This is the crazy love that realizes I have been given a gift I didn't earn or deserve. Isn't this the best kind of gift? If my husband loved me and came home one day with a beautiful diamond and told me he wanted me to have it. Would I tell him I probably haven't earned it, so no thanks? If I earn something and work for it, that is not a gift. And while earning things for quality work is not at all bad, it is not what God is about. It would be insensitive to my husband who thoughtfully brought home something of beauty to refuse the gift.

In a slightly different example, what if my father's company sold for billions of dollars one day, and he called his kids together and told us we all had complete access to his bank account for whatever we needed at any time. We couldn't spend all the money if we tried. Can you imagine telling a friend the next day that you were calling in a $50-debt from a few weeks back when you loaned her some money because she lost her job? Let's look a layer deeper. Would you call in that debt with someone you helped out but had recently betrayed you?

I certainly hope not. When we are given the infinite gift of resources poured into our own lives, the best way to honor that is to be generous to those around us every opportunity we have!

This love we receive from Yeshua is like that kind of resource! It is a love that shows itself by being kind to those who are intentionally cruel to us. It is the love that calls us to pray for blessing on our enemies. It is the love that forgives those that don't deserve or ask for it, and do it quietly without fanfare. It is the love that pours out our lives into our communities, workplaces, and living spaces. It is the greatest love of all.

There is a popular song about the greatest love of all. The song tells us that learning to love ourselves is the greatest love of all. Written by Linda Creed and originally recorded by George Benson in 1977, Whitney Houston topped the charts with her version of it in 1985. Whitney was a beautiful, gifted woman who began her singing career in her church as a child. The song begins with hopeful reminder that children (as Jesus also taught) are our future:

> I believe the children are our are future
> Teach them well and let them lead the way
> Show them all the beauty they possess inside
> Give them a sense of pride to make it easier
> Let the children's laughter remind us how we used to be

Yet as the war ravages our lives, the song follows with this:

> Everybody searching for a hero
> People need someone to look up to
> I never found anyone who fulfill my needs
> A lonely place to be
> And so I learned to depend on me

Yes, we are all searching for a hero. The question men most ask deep in their hearts is *Am I enough?* When it comes down to it, will I stand, am I a hero? And most women come to ask, *Am I lovely? Am I worthy of being saved? Is there a hero who will be worthy of my heart?* So often these questions are left unanswered. And worse, the answers are *no*. There isn't anyone we can depend on here who will always let us in and never let us down, one who values us for who we were created to be, and will tell us our identity in love.

It is a lonely place to be that so many find themselves in as the world rips and tears at our childlike innocence and strikes wounds deep into our hearts that we spend a lifetime seeking a way to heal from.

> I decided long ago
> Never to walk in anyone's shadows
> If I fail, if I succeed
> At least I'll live as I believe
> No matter what they take from me
> They can't take away my dignity

We respond with a hardness, a protective layer. We will not walk in anyone's shadow, and we will follow our heart. We take that sense of pride from verse 1, and we feed it, insisting we will stand on our own merits and pay our own debts. We owe no one. What I find most interesting is that God speaks to these very things. He tells us our own hearts will deceive us but that his wings bring shelter, and we can never lose our dignity with him because we are made in the very image of God, the Creator for great purpose. But we find this purpose in the one who gave us life and our gifts and our very dignity. Honestly, it is exhausting to have to preserve it ourselves, standing alone, refusing to depend on God or anyone else.

> Because the greatest
> Love of all is happening to me
> I found the greatest
> Love of all inside of me
> The greatest love of all
> Is easy to achieve
> Learning to love yourself
> It is the greatest love of all

This is where the journey of the song takes us and also the journey many people find themselves searching for the answers to our deepest brokenness in relationships with others and internally. The answer the world gives is the greatest love of all, learning to love yourself.

It is tricky to sort through this. I've heard well-meaning people ask: But can you love others if you don't love yourself? Haven't we learned that self-care is necessary if we are going to be able to care for others? How can we be able to help others if we are an exhausted mess ourselves?

*Well yes*, I thought. *What about that?*

This is where we break out of the wisdom of the world. The worse answer, of course, is to not love ourselves and be cruel out of that dark place to those around us. And too many people live in that dark place, creating much pain in and around them.

Yet we can see tragically in Whitney Houston's life that even this call to love ourselves is not possible on our own. I never knew her and cannot speak to her own heart, but sadly she died too soon and struggled with drug addiction, eating disorders, and volatile love relationships. From the outside, she appears to be a woman who never found the peace she desperately sought. It seems she never did find her identity even while singing about the greatest love of all—learning to love yourself. It seems she could not make that work for her in the real broken world we exist here and now. Even so she had a foundation of growing up around religious people and organizations from churches to schools. Sometimes this is the most troubling of all. Many think that being engaged in good religious activities mean following God. And one of the most important messages Jesus had when he came to speak personally to us was that religion is not the answer, and it is often the thing that puts us in the most danger. Religion, too often, is a system set in place by humans to earn God's love and pay our own debts, so he will have to come help us out. If self-love and religious obligations won't save us, then what?

Jesus addresses this directly in Matthew 22 and Mark 12.

> "Teacher, which is the greatest command-
> ment in the law?" And Jesus said to him, "You
> shall love the Lord your God with all your heart
> and with all your soul and with all your mind.
> This is the great and first commandment. And a
> second is like it: You shall love your neighbor as
> yourself." (Matthew 22:36–37 ESV)

Notice he doesn't tell them to go to synagogue more. He doesn't tell them to pray longer or to fast or to say Hail Mary or make sure to get baptized. It is good to pray and gather with others who walk the way of Jesus. And fasting is really a given if you study the way of Jesus very long. However, it is made very clear what matters more than anything else. John (who described himself and the one Jesus loved) follows later with deeper explanation about the importance of love:

> So we have come to know and to believe
> the love that God has for us. God is love, and
> whoever abides in love abides in God, and God
> abides in him. By this his love perfected with us
> so that we may have the confidence for the day
> of judgment, because as he is, so also are we in
> this world. There is no fear in love, but perfect
> love casts out fear. For fear has to do with punish-
> ment, and whoever fears has not been perfected
> in love. We love because he first loved us. (1 John
> 4:16–19 ESV)

This is the greatest love of all, that God loved us while we were still confused, lost, detestable, and unclean. We don't clean ourselves up to earn God's love. We accept God's love. And he takes that dirty, stained garment, and he trades it for the white robe of royalty. That is the greatest love, the love that completely unearned we accept and, in doing so, learn our identity as a royal child. His love first fills all that empty space we have been trying to fill with eating, shopping, drinking, drugs, human relationships, success, money, children, good deeds, fame, appreciation, extreme physical events, accomplishments, and on and on. That black hole inside us will never be satisfied until God's love fills it. And though he loves us from before time began, he does not force us to allow the love in. That is our choice.

Once we chose that love, and it fills us, we can't help but reflect back that love to him. We are so full of love that we must love God who changed everything and brought life and fulfillment and grace. Then the unending outpouring of that love overflows onto those around us, our neighbors, our friends, and even those who persecute us. When we allow love like that to take us over, we cannot help but leak it out all around us.

Consider the obsession with self-care. Jesus clearly explained that if we take care of his work, he will take care of our world. There isn't enough self-care or self-help in the universe to match the compassionate love of the Creator to heal and lift us up in his way and time so that we might be equipped to do everything he has called us to do. Imagine if Jesus turned to his friends the night before he was to become the final sacrifice and explained, "Men, I haven't been sleeping well lately. There is a lot of strain on me. I mean, the last time I prayed, I think I was sweating blood. And you were sleeping through it. We are all completely exhausted. I don't think I can do a great job saving all of humanity this worn down and stressed. Let's forgo this 'being captured by Romans' thing and take a little break. I think a villa on the Dead Sea sounds nice for a weekend. We could use some self-care. Let's take care of me for a bit so I can sacrifice my life for the world, feeling a little more like my best self."

Teasing aside, of course, we are of no use to those around us if we are crippled in exhaustion or emotional turmoil. I suppose in a sense, this process is a form of self-care when looked at from a certain angle but not in the way the world directs us. The answer that changes lives is in seeking to rest in the healing and peace of Yeshua. In the case that we are no use to God, ourselves, or anyone—if we are not plugged into our beloved and drinking streams of living water He only provides and eating from the bread of life to sustain each day, if you call that self-care, then truly, yes, that is vital. What I am concerned with is the overwhelming effort the world presses into us that we must "take care of me first," and that is how we love one another better. I see this is a dangerous message and puts us once again where we do not belong—the center of the universe.

When we do seek the living water and bread of life from the hand of our shepherd, he refreshes and strengthens us. I have seen him encourage us to keep working because we haven't exhausted as much as we think, and he wants to see us grow. I've seen him infuse us with new energy to get something finished. But no matter what, he will always provide what we need if we ask.

I have struggled through these questions in my own life. I have been tired of loving others and felt my own love tank getting precariously low. I have asked myself, If this is real, if it is true, do I believe it? I tend toward the extreme, and I have put all my chips in the pot that Yeshua was God speaking to us, and he meant it. He didn't say love and extend grace "up to a certain point." He is clear this way is all the way. It includes laying down your life if called to do so. He does have endless resources. But that doesn't mean that sometimes the transfer isn't intended once in a while to come right on time to find out if we really are willing to risk it all on love. Not once have I been let down. In looking back, I have yet to regret making a decision to love someone else at a cost to me and not seen my Father, Creator, King pour lavish grace upon grace over me exactly when it was most needed to fill me back up with joy and new strength to love again. Maybe these times, when I give until there are only a few drips left my ability to take in this love expands and grows for future grace.

The exception to this, I believe, comes when we are trying to do it in our own strength, when we are choosing our own assignments and making the choices to go where we are not called. In these cases, exhaustion can overtake us, and, mercifully so, that could be what slows us down and stops us enough to ask if we are going off track into our own works and our own plans. This can lead us to dangerous territory because we don't have the long view, all the information. And when we go rogue trying to do good things in our own mind, we can also create problems for the bigger plans we aren't aware of.

If we stay in communication with Him and are working with the love and grace he supplies, we are powerfully equipped to reach those God brings into our lives. This is the greatest love of all.

# Chapter 10

# Assignment

Once we have found enough healing and wholeness to be of use to those around us, once we have some vision to not be one more of the blind leading the blind, once we lay down our own plans and seek directly from the one who made us, we can get to work in the things that will bring us lasting satisfaction and fulfillment. We begin to find out what our assignments will be.

I love the analogy of a great symphony. If everyone comes together to play Beethoven's Ninth Symphony, but one person insists on playing Vivaldi's "Spring," it fundamentally will not work. But if you aren't willing to give up your own ideas and agree to participate in the score the conductor has assigned, there won't be any beauty. If all the symphony musicians brought their own songs to rehearsal, you have a disaster—cacophony, chaos! In order for something beautiful to emerge from one hundred different people, they must submit their freedom to the conductor and follow him. Can you imagine the musician who sues the orchestra because they were fired for not agreeing to perform the conductor's choice of music assignment? When that musician ends up unemployed and homeless, only a fool would sit with him on the street corner and bemoan the rigidity of the symphonic system and the gall of the conductor to take away the individual needs of the musician.

In reality, when we agree to the same score, how we play the notes we are given can be very personal and beautiful. All the same, the orchestra stands as a unit, and the conductor is the one who receives the glory for the performance. He is the one who pulls it all together. The fourth chair, second violin player would look like an arrogant idiot for standing on her chair at the end of the performance, waving her bow and saying, "But look at me, me me!" All the same, every violinist, clarinetist, and the one who plays the triangle is important to creating the majesty. Every chair must be full to make the whole work. Good symphonic musicians are glad to allow the conductor to have the glory and to play their part to the best of their ability no matter how small it may seem. It is vital work!

I never loved symphony orchestra work. I struggle with that whole submission thing, even today. I want to pick the music and be the only one on my part. And chamber music is where I've enjoyed performing the most! It's nice over there with my little group and kingdom. However beautiful chamber music is, it's not nearly as majestic and grand as a Beethoven symphony!

Thankfully, God will even use someone like me. I have come to want his assignment for my life, knowing it will be fun and fulfilling and probably tailor-made for me and my own gifts and experiences.

In joining God's kingdom work, I become one whose name the enemy hates! I want them to cringe when they hear that I am praying, and I am loving those around me, and I'm learning to humble myself and put others first. I am listening more and learning all I can from them and practicing compassion for those I don't understand or agree with. I am a peacemaker and a builder of ruins. They begin to see that no matter what they throw at me, I'm committed to this love until it takes my very life. I want the perfect love that lives bold and fearless. I want to be a danger to the gates of hell!

However, I know I can get excited, and especially early on, I've had to be locked away in my castle garden learning what preparation for assignment means. Thankfully, God has the grace as I'm learning to protect me (and others) from myself. One thing I have learned is that evil is not to be trifled with or underestimated. This is real war and not a game. I must never take on my own ideas, turn them into my own assignments, and go rogue on the commander of the kingdom forces. This is an area where people who want to follow God and do much good can get all tangled up—things that are good but not of God. There are people I want to help, good things I want to jump into, but God has the master plan and vision. I can cause a lot of damage and get myself into trouble running out on my own, looking for all the good things I think need to be done, getting things out of order, putting myself in danger, being in places I wasn't called, business that wasn't mine, and going where I will be unprotected because I am not on assignment. This is another way we end up playing God. Worse damage is done this way: Christians who hurt people in the name of doing good is more harmful than what dark forces do in the name of evil.

Learning to submit is sometimes not going some place you want to help because you are not being called there. This means we have to learn to see and hear where we are being called. In order to be effective, we have to have relationship with the one who gives the assignments and submit to that leadership believing He is good, and he knows better. We may not know the reasons, but we decide to trust that there is an ultimate plan bigger than our short sight and put our hands to what we are called to do. That is also where we will be protected and empowered. It is where we will be the most effective! Even Jesus, here on earth, wasn't out to do whatever he wanted. He stayed connected in prayer to the Father and said he looked out for what his assignment called him to do.

> For I have come down from heaven, not to
> do my own will but the will of him who sent me.
> (John 6:38 ESV)

On my birthday solo retreat where I seek God's voice and spend time in prayer and reading, I spent some time asking him to show me what we would build together. I had finally come to the end of myself and was willing to join his kingdom. I realized that on my own, I was limited at best and destructive at worst, so help me learn to submit. As I prayed and asked about how to help build *his* kingdom instead of mine, I wanted to see and have vision of what we would be doing, what he would ask me to do. "I'm ready to see the blueprint, Father. That's why we're here, right? Give me the score, and show me where I fit in. Here, I'll just come up on the podium with you and look over your shoulder." It was after a day of this that I heard that little whisper helping to reshape my thought process:

> ME: I can't wait to start building with you. What will we do this year? Do you have a blueprint? Show me your vision!
>
> WHISPER: That isn't how it works.
>
> ME: I don't understand. I want to build with you, be part of your project.
>
> WHISPER: You will. But I don't give you the plans in advance.
>
> ME: Oh, of course. I still am getting used to all of this. So I'm not asking the right question yet.
>
> WHISPER: Yes, dear one. You are on your way. I love that you want to partner with me.
>
> ME: Okay then. I trust you have the master plan, and I don't actually have to see what it's going to look like. Can you just point me to where you'd like me to get started and give me my assignment?
>
> WHISPER: Of course! And you've already begun. You are picking up your tools. And as you go, I'll let you know where to get to work and what to do. First there is preparation.
>
> ME: I can't wait till someday I can see with a perspective on what the whole will look like!
>
> WHISPER: Oh, you will! And it will be better than your wildest imagination!

In order to get our assignment, we have to be willing to take whatever it is and do it with all our heart. No job is too small to be beneath us. And no job too large that we can't handle if he sends us. My first job was to learn the cost of forgiveness. To forgive those who hurt me and see the cost of forgiving me is at least as great. It wasn't a particularly fun assignment, but it was vital in my training.

I knew my assignment because I was already spending time every day in prayer. Some people wonder why they don't hear more clearly from God. I cannot answer this because God doesn't exactly tell us the formula. Sure he gives advice on how to love and participate in the relationship, but I can't say why someone else is not feeling they are hearing from God. I do know that we are promised we will find him when we seek with our entire heart. I am suspicious that some who aren't hearing are a bit half-hearted about the search. Since I don't know inside another's heart, it would be a guess. And there are other reasons the communication lines can get stuffed up. If you are seeking to hear from God on something, a few things you might ask are how much time and effort are you putting in seeking. Do you spend more time on social media than in prayer, asking for God's leading? Do you spend more time at the gym? On the phone with friends? Shopping? Watching random YouTube videos? Fill in the blank for you. If so, it's possible you are really more interested in those things than hearing God speak to you. Then decide honestly: are you seeking with your whole heart, or are you mildly curious? You are willing to hear him out, but first he will have to break through all the truly important things to you.

When I turned this direction, my heart had changed, and I came to see this was actually the most important thing. I prayed often through a day. I began fasting days when I felt the move to get serious. And every time I felt hungry, instead of eating food, I would be reminded to pray about what was pressing me for an answer. I read voraciously the Bible texts with my ear to the page asking, "What does it say to me today?" I worked out thoughts with like-minded friends and mentors I trusted. I searched old messages from teachers I respected that might have a connection. I was asking for guidance and willing to do whatever I was called to, and the information I needed always came. It came in podcasts. It came in devotional emails. It came from Bible apps. It came from seeing things play out in the world around me with new eyes. It came in the whispers of my heart in times of quiet stillness. It came in dreams. It came in discussion with other like-minded Jesus-following, trusted friends. Sometimes it even came from "secular" sources around me.

I knew forgiveness was my big assignment at the time. It took heart work and deep change. It took study and processing. It took action and deciding to do things before I felt like doing them with the faith that it was right, and my heart would follow (it did in time). It took way more time than I would have agreed to if he would have told me up front. Yet we also have smaller scope but equally vital assignments too. While learning about forgiveness was taking me months, then a year (and this is certainly not a finished subject), I also would be called to send a card of encouragement to a friend or take extra time to listen to someone who crossed my path that day or hold my tongue when something sarcastic really begged to be expressed. Sometimes my assignment was to write a blog, and sometimes it was not to write about something or to wait for wider perspective. Sometimes it was to find joy on a wooded trail with a friend and a horse, and sometimes it was to cry on my living room floor for help when I felt wounded and lost.

Earlier in my life, I tried to stuff Jesus in the trunk and drive myself because I didn't want his assignments. I wanted to call my own moves. I was afraid he might send me to Africa instead of getting to pursue my own personal goals. Today I see that His assignments are the most engaging, the most fulfilling, and tailor-made to bring me exactly the struggles that I'll learn and grow from and at the same time bring me to the places I most desperately want to see. I was excited when one assignment took me to a Maya city in Mexico's Yucatán to bring food and clothes to people living in poverty and serve painting houses and handing out eye glasses, playing my violin for children, and telling them stories about what it means to be the friend of God. Yet while I was there enjoying sunshine during winter and laughing with children, I also yearned for something more. And today I am always on the lookout for the possible assignment to Africa or anywhere I am needed to bring light into darkness! The irony is that I'm now ready to go wherever I'm called, and I haven't gotten the assignment to Africa yet.

I felt like Christine Caine's daughter in a story I once heard her tell. They were in a large store picking up all kinds of necessities, and her daughter asked if she could buy a small flashlight. As they went through the checkout and were getting ready to leave the store, the daughter was turning on the light and was concerned it didn't seem to be working very well. Christine explained to her they were in the store with lots of light everywhere so the light was working, but you can't tell because there is light all around. So the daughter replied, "Mommy! Let's go find some darkness!"

# Chapter 11

# Resistance

A life centered in the love of Yeshua turns us into lighthouses to anyone seeking refuge. When we follow in his way, we live a life opposite of most of the world's messages. We should look different. While Yeshua was here, he assured us that just as he suffered for choosing love, we also will suffer for this. The dark forces that have temporary rule here are real and strong. When you refuse to enlist with them or even consider a peace treaty, you are guaranteed to become a target. We move from existing only on the seen realm to the unseen. We begin to get our minds off the things of man and begin to hunger for the things of God. We stop doing simply earthly good and begin to participate in the eternal good.

I specifically chose the phrase "eternal good" because we can do plenty of temporary good that has short-term earthly impact and still be relatively harmless for the things that change eternity. This is where evil is most effective. If the darkness can keep men and women focused on their own self-directed assignments around them that they see as good, they can be too distracted to ask or engage in what God is trying to do through them. Doing short-term earthly good things are beautiful, and I'm not discouraging that. Do lots of small acts of kindness. Donate to causes you believe in, and volunteer at a homeless shelter. Foster unwanted animals or even unwanted children if you are able to do that well! And in doing these, you may be doing some massive eternal impact as well. The knife edge is always in the heart. If you are doing your life—including these kind of beautiful things—with Yeshua as the core, if you are seeking his voice and his plans above your own and dancing in step with his symphony, if he is the one directing your steps and filling your life, then you are unquestionably engaged in things that impact eternity. If you are doing things you see as good to be a better person or to redeem that empty place in your heart or because they secretly make you feel superior to your neighbors or in order to put God in your debt so he owes you a good life, then doing good things actually become a deceptive way of running away from God. If your life of good things flows from any other reason than the love that is flowing through your healed, restored, living heart submitted each day to God's plan, then the good you are doing very likely has a short-term localized effect. You are limiting yourself. This message is a hard one, but I didn't write it.

> "Why do you call me good?" Jesus answered. "No one is good except God alone." (Mark 10:18 NIV)

> To the pure, all things are pure, but to the defiled and unbelieving, nothing is pure; both their minds and their consciences are defiled. They profess to know God, but they deny him by their works. They are detestable, disobedient, unfit for any good work. (Titus 1:15–16 NIV)

> We sinned; in our sins we have been a long time, and shall we be saved? We have all become like one who is unclean, and all our righteous deeds are like a polluted garment. We all fade like a leaf, and our iniquities, like the wind, take us away. (Isaiah 64:5b–6 NIV)

These writings are saying that none of us are good enough, and our best deeds and works on our own are detestable and like a dirty robe. Actually, a dirty robe is a euphemism. Some translations try to get closer to the original, which is more closely a used menstrual pad. That's some serious language meant to shake us up into thinking about this radically. Through our western cultural goggles that champion self-esteem and self-love, we are told we simply need to dig deep into our souls to find the beauty and truth within. This message is being slammed here with language so strong that it borders on the foul. Please do not miss this, do not sugarcoat it. This message is dangerous and polarizing. It goes against all the worldly way to entice us with.

> I am the vine; you are the branches. If you remain in me and I in you, you will bear much fruit; apart from me, you can do nothing. (John 15:5 NIV)

This is black-and-white clear. Jesus says anything we do on our own is actually nothing. We cannot and are not expected to engage in eternal good and take on the powers of darkness on our own human ability. When we do, we look great to the people around us. But God who sees the heart isn't fooled. Regardless if our heart is to earn God's favor (which he clearly says we cannot do because he already loves us completely) or if we do it to make ourselves look better than others, the acts are disgusting to him. And in the end, when he is looking at the books of our lives—those things burn away in the refining fire. But the things we do out of love for Yeshua—because he loves us and calls us to love each other, those things stand the fire and are refined like a pure gold, and they have eternal value.

At first it sounds confusing and negative. But digging down a layer, it is exciting and amazing. We are given the opportunity as mortal creatures to have an impact on eternal things! Know in advance: There is a price. Nothing this good is unopposed by darkness. It is one thing to understand this in the mind and another thing entirely to experience it for yourself. The greatest weapon darkness has is fear and intimidation. Remember, even the prince of darkness doesn't hold his own keys. The gates of hell cannot stand against us because Yeshua gave his life in self-sacrifice, and now the gates cannot be secured. Do not be surprised, dear one, that if you step out to live in this beautiful and powerful way full of light, you will meet resistance.

It is real. It is personal.

The God-man who came here with the intent of bringing a lifeline to the hearts of all humanity had a mountaintop experience or two himself. When Jesus met John, the one baptizing people in repentance to prepare their hearts for God's huge work of that time, he was baptized as a symbol of his coming death. And those who were there heard the very voice of God, his Father, saying that he was pleased with his son. The Holy Spirit descended visibly that day, and God's presence was palpable. After this, Jesus went into the desert for forty days where the prince of darkness himself met him in an attempt to confuse, tempt, and deter his path. Yes, even the son of God met resistance as he walked through this enemy territory. I am grateful my impact isn't at the level of having to meet the very prince of darkness face-to-face. I like to think we humans start off pretty harmless at first, and the lower-level minions get to try their hand with those beginning their journey. Over time, our levels of attack and resistance grow as we are more effective. I suppose, in general, the more difficult the resistance we meet, the more important the assignment.

As I walked into my assignments, I wasn't ready for the battles that would come. I'm not certain anything can adequately prepare someone for this, except going through it. Still it helps to know to expect it, otherwise you may find yourself wounded and stranded, exposed on the field, not knowing what happened or what to do about it. I have been there.

There would be days of amazing insight, powerful connections, encouragement into someone's life that had an impact I could have not realized in advance. We don't always see the importance of an assignment in this line of living. Something that seems on the surface insignificant can be the mustard seed that produces the largest tree in time. In fact, God delights in these paradoxes. We don't always know what a kind word to a stranger meant. I've heard of lives saved because the message in a simple greeting was the exact words someone needed to hear to decide not to end their life that day. There are no small assignments in this work. We are called to trust and answer the call even if we don't understand at the time how it could be meaningful.

After a fantastic top of the mountain personal word from God into my heart or being used to do something beautiful for someone I would often find myself descending in turmoil, feeling like I shouldn't leave the house and talk to people, I say things that do not come out right. I still have selfish motives that surface. I become convinced everything is just in my head, some kind of coping tool for a difficult time in my life. I cannot go on suddenly questioning everything I was certain of only hours ago. The messages were personally geared toward my doubts and weakness: You are too much. You are not enough. No one will ever love you for who you are. You've been rejected. Who could even like someone like you? Tone yourself down so people can stand being around you! Your future will be sad and lonely. Why did you say that to her? You're a hypocrite. What do you know anyway?

The messages are personally chosen for each of us. But the common theme is to bully us to duck down, shut up, play it safe, protect ourselves, cower in fear, and doubt what God spoke to us. If we can't be held in our prison cell, at least they can try to keep us from storming the fortress, daring to bring freedom and light to others too weak to stand for themselves.

I began to recognize the pattern—mountaintop, valley of the shadow of death, mountaintop, valley, mountaintop, valley. I began to ask myself if I was unstable. I had found the way of Yeshua. So why was my world such a wave curve of high and low? One comfort I found was in the Psalms. David would write things to praise the God who delivered him from the fowler's snare and set his feet on a rock and then ask in the next chapter, "Why are you downcast, oh, my soul?" and say things like, "A day in your presence is better than a thousand years without you," and then "Adonai, look away from me so I may have peace before I die." If David was a man after God's own heart, at least it seemed I was in good company.

Once the attack was so severe, I actually was on my living room floor in sobs that shook my entire body. Out loud, when I could breathe enough to speak, I remember saying, "I am done. I'm wounded. and I don't even know what happened."

> WHISPER. Beloved, get up.
> ME. I can't. I really can't. I don't know what happened, but I cannot move. I need help.
> WHISPER. Listen to me. You are okay, I'm here.
> ME [choking on my own breath]. Help. I need help. You have to get me out of here. I can't hear you!
> WHISPER. Can you hear me now?
> ME. Help me. I will die here. Why would you leave me here?
> WHISPER [louder and louder]. Listen to me. I am here. Can you hear me?
> ME. [Silence.]

I was sure, if I wasn't carried off to a safe place, I probably would die. And I didn't even understand why at this point. Something caught me deep, unaware, from behind. The attack was stealthy and effective. Though I was physically "safe" in my own living room, I was acutely aware that in the spiritual realm, I had been seriously ambushed. I probably had been enjoying a lovely mountaintop and had neglected my armor.

> WHISPER. *I am here. Listen to me. I have you. You are going to be fine. Can you hear me. Open your ears and breathe. I am right here.*

I was certain after that time that Yeshua was right there with me, and I was so spinning in darkness that I couldn't gain my head. It was like a horrible chaotic noise was the only awareness I had. Darkness raged in my own head. Panic overtook me, and I couldn't hear. But I had an impression of him kneeling next to me calmly but firmly talking to me to bring me back: *I am here. Can you hear me? Choose to hear my voice. You can choose.*

It reminds me of Peter when he jumped out of the boat so excited to walk on water, and then the storm caught his attention, and he began to sink. Jesus reached down and pulled him up—mountaintop, valley. The light compelled him to risk, to jump out of the boat! Amazing mountaintop of walking on the water followed directly by sinking under the waves. What got into you, Peter? The darkness. He lost his faith and lost his nerve as his attention was drawn to the wind and storm. Maybe he began to hear the voices, reminding him he was crazy. "People don't walk on water. This makes no sense! What do you think you're doing? You are going to die here. Did he really call you out here, or are you out of line on your own? You aren't God. You should stay in the boat where humans belong!" Peter began to go under, desperately needing to be pulled up. The best news is Yeshua will *always* reach down and pull us up. Still we must learn to stand firm, eyes locked with his, and have the nerve to love without fear. One thing I know about Peter, about myself—we tend toward compulsive, reactive, and probably need help more often than others, prone to wander for sure. But at least we're getting out of the boat.

The band Mumford & Sons has a great song that reminds me of these truths, and the lines excerpted from *Hopeless Wanderer* have inspired me many days:

> I wrestled long with my youth
> We tried so hard to live in the truth
> But do not tell me all is fine
> When I lose my head, I lose my spine
>
> So when your hopes on fire
> But you know your desire
> Don't hold a glass over the flame
> Don't let your heart grow cold

I will call you by name
I will share your road
But hold me fast, hold me fast
'Cause I'm a hopeless wanderer

I too wrestled long with my youth, going my own way, and struggling with the truth. And I have seen direct evidence that I will be taken down when I lose my head. I have learned to hold to truth against the screaming messages of darkness intended to stop any progress of bringing that flame of hope into the world of darkness. Faith is never about letting go of my analytical mind or dropping my head and following my heart. You must keep your head. You must be rooted deeply in truth in order to guide your heart.

I have hopes and dreams and a deep desire to bring light and love to the world around me. I hope you do too! Don't hold a glass over your flame or let your heart grow cold as the opposition comes. Yeshua calls us by name, and he walks with us and shares the road as our closest companion. I know I need him to reach down and pull me up when I start to sink. I need the shepherd to come with his staff and nudge my wandering sheep self back to the path I am supposed to be on.

I am slightly more battle seasoned today. I now find the mountaintop-valley life is somewhat predictable. And though the mountains are just as glorious when he speaks or moves in a way I see and hear. I am less surprised by the ambush attacks that come after. When disruption or doubt and fear show up, I know their voice, and I know the name that is greater. In fact, I've begun to almost enjoy riding that wave today…almost. One thing is for sure, God promises to work all things together for the good of those who love him and are called to his purposes. This means that no matter how bad the attack looks, there is an opportunity in it if I bring it to Yeshua for counterattack. I might get wounded. It isn't always fun. But I'm not taken out nearly as fatally as before. All the same, I never want to become overconfident! Evil is not to be trifled with. And as I grow, so does the level of opposition. When you are basically living a harmless life, you don't need the opposition of a cunning high-level master of deception to keep you from setting others free. Once you become effective, the opposition of resistance must also step up the game. Today when push back or resistance comes, I pause to look at what I've done lately. Something I might have taken for granted could have made a larger impact than I realized. Of course, I also pause to check in because resistance can also come when I am going off track as well, and that isn't a force of evil. It's the kindness of God pushing me back as I begin to wander. The answer is always turn to God, which is the whole point anyway. Conversation and relationship are the key, not going it alone. No matter what, when the struggle comes, now I know that it will pass.

# Chapter 12

# Counterattack

For we do not wrestle against flesh and blood but against the rulers, against the authorities, against the cosmic powers over this present darkness, against the spiritual forces of evil in the heavenly places.

—Ephesians 6:12 ESV

The most important thing you can do as often as you remember, and certainly if you feel an attack, is to pray on your armor! For we do not wrestle with flesh and blood. If you took only this message away from this book, it would change your life for the better. Your spouse, your mom, your boss, that woman in the office—they are not your enemy. We have an enemy. But the enemy you face is *not* flesh and blood. Your enemy is the prince of darkness and all agents of darkness who want to cause disruption, anger, fear, jealousy, envy, pride. This cycle takes away our God-given freedom, and we now have the knowledge and the power to stop the cycle. We can choose love, forgiveness, grace, and stop the madness. We bring the power of the Creator's kingdom of life.

Therefore, take up the whole armor of God
that you may be able to withstand in the evil day
and having done all to stand firm. Stand, there-

fore, having fastened on the belt of truth and having put on the breastplate of righteousness and, as shoes for your feet, having put on the readiness given by the gospel of peace. In all circumstances, take up the shield of faith with which you can extinguish all the flaming darts of the evil one; and take the helmet of salvation and the sword of the Spirit, which is the word of God. (Ephesians 13–17 ESV)

This became a regular practice for me. Notice the armor is protective and defensive for the most part. The only offensive piece of the armor is the sword, and that comes last. George Washington was first recorded to have said, "The best offensive is a good defense." Defensive power is where it all begins.

The armor we are told to choose to put on every day begins with truth. Truth is continually washed away the farther we move in history from the word (Yeshua) being here, walking and teaching on this earth with us. Today the popular culture message is there is no truth, and everyone is encouraged to claim their own personal truth.

Logically, this is problematic for me. The statement that there is no absolute truth in itself is a truth claim. If everyone must choose their own truth for themselves, then there is no comprehensive encompassing truth. If that is the case that truth claims are unreliable as a rule, then how can someone tell me there is *not* an absolute truth? It is insanity if you dig through the analytical layers. This isn't rational at all. It is akin to intellectual schizophrenia. Following Yeshua never requires a loss of logic and willful blindness to the laws the universe was created on.

Regardless, I can understand wanting to believe there is no absolute truth. It feels much easier on the surface; it is less divisive and allows us to keep a kind of peace. Sadly, it is a lie, a false peace. Is it possibly even a dangerous peace? It is observable that some things are absolutely true. And not explaining that truth is deadly to the people around us if they have not learned for themselves. They may not want to hear the truth and decide to avoid speaking to us, but do we carry responsibility for their demise because it was easier to be nice than to tell the truth? Always keep in mind, love is required. Speaking truth to someone struggling can only be done in love. Truth must be married to love, or no matter how right you are, it will still be destructive. In fact, truth without love can be the most destructive force in the universe.

Gravity is a reality we all must live by. I didn't create it. If a friend told me of a plan to fly unassisted off a cliff, it would be irresponsible of me to encourage her to find her own truth and see what happens. It may hurt their feelings if I seem unsupportive of her dream, but I must risk losing the friendship if I love the person. Again, the delivery of the truth must be in love. People do not care how much you know until they know how much you care. Of course, if she heard me out and assured me that the law of gravity is an interesting concept, but she needs to find her own truth, I would still love her as much as I ever did. In practice, this is not this simple or obvious. There are things we are still studying to understand. Science has proven limited over history. Prevailing opinions can be built on incomplete data or a narrow view of a complex issue. Yet the very existence of the scientific method is the search for understanding of a world created on principles that can be duplicated and relied on. The universe runs in a consistent and observable way under the laws in which it was created—truth. We may not completely understand it, but the fact that we pursue the laws of the universe is because we believe they exist and should be understood so we can live better lives.

We also have a responsibility to seek out truths in the spiritual, unseen world. The physical world is a representation. We can see patterns and understand that there is a parallel underpinning of an unseen realm that comes before the physical. By the time, something is observed in the physical realm. It has already been set into place in the unseen realm.

By the time cancer is detected in a medical test, it has already been working unseen in where we cannot see with our physical realm tools and systems. By the time the parents see a teenager lost in a drug addiction, there were unseen shifts in the heart and mind, setting that course of direction. If we could understand the truth of this, it would make us more effective in living better lives and helping others find more peace, stability, and well-being. Yeshua taught of this principle while he walked with us:

> You have heard that it was said to those of old, "You shall not murder; and whoever murders will be liable to judgment." But I say to you that everyone who is angry with his brother will be liable to judgment. (Matthew 5:21–22 ESV)

> You have heard that it was said, "You shall not commit adultery." But I say to you that everyone who looks at a woman with lustful intent has already committed adultery with her in his heart. (Matthew 5:27–28 ESV)

He is explaining that murder begins with anger nurtured in the heart unseen; and adultery begins with a look in lust that you can hide from those around you. Both of these can be hidden and made light of. This is how people end up in places they would never have believed, one unchecked thought of the heart at a time. The deeper level of the unseen heart's shifts are what take us eventually to dark places. We like to think the slippery slope argument is not applicable to us. Wanting a second look at that woman doesn't make a man guilty of an affair, does it? Have you ever noticed the guilty person who hasn't committed the offense in the physical but has begun the process in their own mind plead, "I haven't done anything wrong!"? Nurturing those little vengeful scenes in your mind can feel good at the time. It's harmless, right? There are many steps, many points still "harmless" to stop along that process. This is true. However, when we plant a tiny seed and then secretly nurture, feed, and water it, how are we so surprised when it grows, and eventually, we end up with an unmanageable tree. Once the tree is established, we have to keep pruning it back but never seem to get the stump and root removed because it is not in our own power. At this point, a much more serious removal method is required. It is not easy to release your anger and take self-control to not look twice and then nurture little fantasies in your heart, yet this is still a better place to combat murder and betrayal than when the weapon is in your hand, or the door is closed behind you.

The point is there are laws the universe operates upon, and the seen things have an unseen spiritual underpinning that can be understood gradually, more clearly, as we make the effort to observe and learn. Just as we should explore physical science and tell people that gravity will take you down even if you can't see it and don't believe it, we should learn about the realities of the spiritual world and the lies that keep people from thriving and could eventually kill them on a level that is as real as the hand in front of your face but not observable with the same eyes. This is the reality of truth.

We are told to begin our armor with truth. We have begun to understand and continue to expand that belt of truth so it can encircle our garments entirely. Without the belt of truth, we are walking around this world of unseen things basically naked and exposed. None of the rest of the armor can help if we can't even keep our clothes on with the belt of truth. No wonder the darkness would prefer to convince you there is no need for a belt. You are vulnerable to any message and can be whipped around by the winds of how you feel at the time. You will believe anything that sounds good. If you don't believe there exists a truth that can be chased after and uncovered over time, then you have little hope to actually finding it. Similarly in science, we don't actually get to make it up as we see fit. This would be akin to not believing the universe functions on observable and repeatable laws but is different for each person, so why have any kind of science because we can all simply smile and say, "Yes, water boils at 212F for you. But don't try to tell me what temperature it boils for me. Today we would consider that insanity. Yet it is exactly what we do about spiritual realm understanding."

In the same vein, someone is welcome to tell me that water boils at 100F, and I can either believe them (do I trust the source), or I can do an experiment and find out for myself. We have a responsibility to seek the truth and the way to life. I would say it is our greatest responsibility here on this earth and will bring us the most fulfillment and well-being for ourselves and those around us. In that journey, God has made a promise that if we will set aside our previous biases of the fact, let's say that we *want* water to boil at 100F, that we will find the truth.

The deeper I have dug into the truth of Yeshua and the living Creator God, the clearer the evidence becomes. And I find it observable in my life and the lives around me. The deeper I dig, the less contradictions I find in the words of God, and the more intellectual schizophrenia exists in human-made religious and philosophical systems, including the practice of atheism. Once the fact that truth does exist becomes clear, then we can begin to put on this armor that keeps us from being mortally wounded by life or having to hide away in a protected space because we are too vulnerable to venture into the battlefield.

Next comes the breastplate of righteousness. The breastplate covers the heart and lungs. This area contains vital organs necessary for life. We can be hit in an arm or leg and continue on, but the center of our being is covered under the breastplate. We accept the righteousness from Yeshua, our defender and the one who paid the penalty we deserved. There are attacks from voices that attempt to pierce my heart by reminding me of my weaknesses and imperfections. They try to kill my heart with messages that I'm selfish, I've hurt people, and deserve to be hurt in return. The messages are always personal attacks sent straight toward those sensitive nerve places in our hearts that if allowed through can take us out quickly. We must put on the righteousness given by Yeshua to deflect those messages. We then are able to use the greater truth of God that we are chosen, called, and have great purpose for good. And these lies can be turned back, and our hearts are protected.

The shoes of peace have been one of my most personally illustrated armor pieces over time. I have had dreams of putting on beautiful white shoes that I loved, and well-meaning friends have told me they are unstylish and unbecoming. I have dreamed of being engaged in a race and taken out by deep mud, knowing in the dream it was because I didn't have the right shoes on. I have come to understand over time that it wasn't only peace with others that my shoes of the gospel were useful for in running forward in my own race but also the peace that allows me to stand confident and still without fear or anxiety, no matter what the world around me appears. The gospel message, in the simplest form, is that I am worse than I ever realized on my own and still loved and valued more than I'd ever hoped by the one who is greatest of all, the one who made the universe and all that is in it, and sustains it every second. In this, I can rest completely, and I can also walk into anything.

The shield of faith defends me from the flaming darts shot at me from a distance. As I grow in seeking truth and understanding, my faith grows as well. The larger my shield becomes and the more strength I have to hold it up, the less vulnerable I am to the flaming darts the dark forces shoot my way. Once again, if I didn't accept that there is a truth we can seek out, I could never grow faith built on the very spiritual scientific method of accumulating knowledge and then experimenting with trial and error. Many say they cannot seem to have faith, but they exercise faith every day and don't even realize it. Darkness tries to convince us that faith is about blindly accepting something you cannot understand or know. That is never what God asked of anyone. He asks for us to engage our brains and to make an effort to learn. Science is much more faith than most want to admit. We make a hypothesis based of previous understanding. We do some experiments to observe what happens, and then we get enough data to move forward. Sometimes we are correct and move onto solid footing. Sometimes we have incomplete assessment. And as we move that way, we find cracks in the ice and dead ends and have to backtrack or adjust. All these steps take various amounts of faith. And once you begin to find solid footing, you can trust the process. Your understanding grows and so does your faith in the future process. God never calls us to shut down the minds he gave us and believe in something with zero evidence. However, we will never move forward out of our small safe areas without using the process of faith to push the edges and grow. Some of us grow in leaps and some in inches as our personality and tolerance allows.

When Yeshua was discovered—or not discovered—at the tomb, when he didn't do what most people expect a dead person to do—

stay dead—there were different reactions from his friends. Some ran to see for themselves. Some jumped to conclusions (maybe the body was stolen or moved). Some remembered Jesus talking about his own death and resurrection and jumped for joy. And some, like Thomas, got stuck in doubts.

> So the other disciples told him, "We have seen the Lord." But he [Thomas] said to them, "Unless I see in his hands the mark of the nails and place my finger into the mark of the nails and place my hand into his side, I will never believe." (John 20:25 ESV)

Thomas didn't get berated for his doubts. Jesus didn't tell him he was a sorry excuse of a disciple for struggling with small faith. He always meets us where we are if we honestly ask him to.

> Eight days later, his disciples were inside again, and Thomas was with them. Although the doors were locked, Jesus came and stood among them and said, "Peace be with you." Then he said to Thomas, "Put your finger here, and see my hands; and put out your hand, and place it in my side. Do not disbelieve but believe." Thomas answered him, "My Lord and my God!" Jesus said to him, "Have you believed because you have seen me? Blessed are those who have not seen and yet have believed." (John 20:26–29 ESV)

Notice it was over a week later before Thomas had his questions answered. I have remained wounded and feeling exposed sitting in doubt longer than I would like at times. God will always meet us where we are. But he doesn't always come on our time line. Thomas did want to believe but was stuck. I know this because when he did see the scars, he had what he needed and stepped a few inches into faith. There were many who saw, but their hearts were hard and blind, and they did not believe. One more evidence of the unseen deep heart realm having so much power—there is great scientific evidence for some things that men and women do not want to believe, and no evidence will ever change their minds. It is the same with faith.

Next comes the helmet which is equated with salvation. Considering how vital protecting the head is, I find it interesting where it comes in the list. Apparently, the helmet is generally put on last. In a physical battle, we know our bodies cannot continue if a fatal blow comes to the brain. The brain is the center of where function through our physical bodies is controlled. Though the breastplate of righteousness covers many vital organs, even more so, the helmet covering the head is imperative because the organs cannot function without the brain for long. Also, for these most vital protections, they are both given by Yeshua to us. Righteousness is not ours to earn, it's given and must be accepted. Salvation is also given to us, and it is connected to his righteousness just as our own brains and vital organs are connected. Yet we must focus and keep our minds fixed in order to keep our heads in battle. Righteousness covers the heart, but salvation covers the mind.

Over time, I have come to know something which was obvious and plain to me. Then, voices of doubt come asking me to question what I have known so clearly. It begins in my mind where I make a choice to "always remember to never forget." I must speak to myself and remember what I have been told, no matter how things appear or what voices attack the ground I've gained. I was there when my hero carried me out of darkness, yet voices still attempt to convince me it never happened. Thoughts echo internally that I'm not worth saving, "Wasn't the prison nice? You knew the routine there. You were safe there." Pay close attention to what your thoughts become fixed on because your heart will eventually follow. We do have control of our thoughts. What enters our minds can come without invitation. But what do we answer ourselves with? What do we feed? We can question our thoughts. We can speak back to the ones that are deceptive. We control this. And once again, truth is key. What we feed in our minds and what we take in are the first line of defense to how healthy our hearts can be. I will always remember my mother saying as I grew up, "Garbage in, garbage out."

> Finally, whatever is true, whatever is honorable, whatever is just, whatever is pure, whatever is lovely, whatever is commendable, if there is any excellence, if there is anything worthy of praise, think about these things. (Philippians 4:8 ESV)

Last of all, we come to the only offensive piece of armor we are given: The sword of the spirit of the word of God. How fascinating that in English we can add the "s" to word and get "sword." We are told that Yeshua is known as the word become flesh:

> In the beginning was the Word, and the Word was with God, and the Word was God. He was in the beginning with God. (John 1:1 ESV)

> And the Word became flesh and dwelt among us, and we have seen his glory, glory as of the only Son from the Father, full of grace and truth. (John 1:14 ESV)

This makes it abundantly clear to me that it is Yeshua who fights for me. The spirit of God is where my offensive power lies. I also contend that, in the upside down world of how we are called to live, the sword should always be first used in our own hearts as we allow Yeshua to work in us before we ever get out to the battlefield.

> For the word of God is living and active, sharper than any two-edged sword, piercing to the division of soul and of spirit, of joints and of marrow, and discerning the thoughts and intentions of the heart. (Hebrews 4:12 ESV)

I pray that God would use that sword, his word, to discern the thoughts and intentions of my own heart first and walk me through them in his gentle surgical way. If this process happens before I head out into the battle, I have understanding that will enable me to be effective. When I walk in truth, righteousness, peace, faith, and salvation, I am then called to responsible use of my sword. Too often, Christians use the sword to cut people into pieces. But Yeshua calls us to use the word to save lives and protect others, not destroy them. Fundamentally, the shoes of peace should carry us everywhere, knowing we do not have to win every single fight, and we can trust the word to do his work in hearts without us slashing each other to a bloody mess, forgetting it is not flesh and blood we are called to fight. The sword is an amazing weapon against the powers of darkness, and that is where it is rightly used.

Consider these things each day intentionally, and do not be surprised when trial and attacks come after times of life, healing, and hearing the whisper in your heart. Do not fear them either. Pray on your armor, and move into your assignments with great expectation because we know the end of the story already. This story has a happy ending for those who chose the true King, and we get to participate in the greatest story that all good stories are fashioned after.

# Chapter 13

# Proof

If they live long enough, people seem to realize they are seeking something, whether it be God—meaning, purpose, truth, or a vague sense of something bigger than themselves. The other side of that coin is that God is desperately seeking us. There are many stories Yeshua told of the joy of recovering something lost: a lost coin, a lost sheep, a lost son. Some are lost for a short time. They wander astray only far enough to see the cliffs of despair and scamper back to the herd with a little fright of what might have happened, relieved to find the shepherd waiting to include them in the herd. Others run headlong off the cliffs, crash down the canyon, and then try to drown themselves in the stream before the shepherd catches up to them, usually having to club them to stun them temporarily, tie up their feet, and carry them back to safety. The smarter sheep finally begin to call out for help. But usually, it's not until they are cast down, which in shepherd language means they've fallen in a way they cannot get right without help, and they will die in a matter of hours. I'm sure the helpless little creature can't think straight to realize the shepherd has been seeking to return the sheep to rights since it first ran toward the cliffs.

This reminds me of another C. S. Lewis moment in his book, *The Silver Chair*. Eustace and Jill found themselves in trouble at school. And in desperation, Eustace calls out to the character of the great lion (representing Yeshua), Aslan. They are pulled into the magical land of Narnia on that cry for help, and Jill is confused as this is her first time out of her own world. The great lion gives her a task to complete that begins the adventure (we always have an assignment). And in her confusion, we read:

> "Please, what task, Sir?" asks Jill.
>
> "The task for which I called you and him here out of your own world," says the lion.
>
> This response puzzles Jill. Nobody called them. They called out to—Somebody—a name she wouldn't know. Wasn't it she and Eustace who asked to come?
>
> "You would not have called to me unless I had been calling to you," says the lion. (C. S. Lewis, *The Silver Chair*)

The deeper truth is we are the ones being called, drawn in to him. He is desperate to recover his beloved treasure—us. We are often confused as the process begins just as Jill was. God has been speaking into our lives for a long time before we begin to hear the voice for ourselves. We can get stuck, feeling like we are crazy to imagine a Creator of the universe is actually calling us out. We have lived so long in the matrix, so to speak, that we question anything outside of that framework. We want proof because that leap of faith seems like a perilous jump into the abyss. In order to let go and accept the assignment, we want some assurance this is not just a strange dream, my imagination, pinning everything on the hope there is more.

Back to *The Silver Chair*, Jill now has to take her assignment and be sent into the new world she's found herself. I love how this entrance is off the edge of a cliff, the leap of faith. But at this point she is out of options.

> "You will have no time to spare," said the lion. "That is why I must send you at once. Come. Walk before me to the edge of the cliff."

[Jill] did as she was told. It was very alarming walking back to the edge of the cliff, especially as the lion did not walk with her but behind her—making no noise on his soft paws.

But long before she had got anywhere near the edge, the voice behind her said, "Stand still. In a moment, I will blow.

The voice had been growing softer toward the end of this speech, and now it faded away altogether. Jill looked behind her. To her astonishment, she saw the cliff already more than a hundred yards behind her and the lion himself, a speck of bright gold on the edge of it. She had been setting her teeth and clenching her fists for a terrible blast of lion's breath; but the breath had really been so gentle that she had not even noticed the moment at which she left the earth. And now there was nothing but air for thousands upon thousands of feet below her.

She felt frightened only for a second. For one thing, the world beneath her was so very far away that it seemed to have nothing to do with her. For another, floating on the breath of the lion was so extremely comfortable. She found she could lie on her back or on her face and twist any way she pleased, just as you can in water (if you've learned to float really well). And because she was moving at the same pace as the breath, there was no wind, and the air seemed beautifully warm. It was not in the least like being in an aeroplane because there was no noise and no vibration. If Jill had ever been in a balloon, she might have thought it more like that, only better. (C. S. Lewis, *The Silver Chair*)

This is how it is with the lion of Judah. What looks fun and entertaining and good to us on the human perspective often leads to dead ends at best and addictions and destruction at worst, But what looks like jumping off a cliff to our peril—when it is God who is calling us to trust him—ends up actually floating on warm breath being set down into our next assignment in undeserved grace. Yet it is not unrealistic to look for signs that it is indeed the Creator King calling us to go. When Thomas (sometimes known as the doubter) questions Yeshua in our Bible text, he is answered with truth, not scorn. We are never called to follow mindlessly, yet the proof we think we want isn't actually what we need.

How many people suggest if God would only "fill in the blank here" then I would believe. Heal my daughter. Turn water into wine for the dinner party tonight. Send me a million dollars to fix my financial problems. Make it rain. Make it not rain. Get me out of this mess. Strangely enough, when he walked on the earth, he did these things in plain sight. Some believed, but some did not believe. It wasn't proof their hearts needed. He not only raised a stinking corpse four days in the grave, but he predicted his own death and resurrection and then pulled that off exactly as he said it would happen. What else does anyone need? Many people have dug into historical records and find overwhelming evidence that this event happened exactly as it is recorded in Bible texts. Yet even in the time when Jesus appeared after his death in front of people, Matthew 28:17 reads, And when they saw him, they worshipped him, but some doubted.

Even seeing doesn't mean believing. This is because it's not a simple matter of evidence and proof. There is more to a woman than her mind, there is also a heart. In our hearts, we struggle against the darkness that says we have to see something to believe it. Yet even in seeing it, we can disbelieve because our hearts cannot let go of something we are holding on to. If Yeshua is truly God in human form, our hearts know that jumping off that cliff means everything changes.

God knows this. He didn't send us a foolproof argument of his identity. He didn't leave a mathematical proof. No matter what our minds tell us, we need more than proof. So he did so much more, he sent a person—not just any person—he came himself. Love came to touch our hearts. He *is* the proof. And now that his spirit lives through us, the ones who call him friend and beloved, we are the proof. We become that love.

> And you show that you are a letter from Christ delivered by us, written not with ink but with the spirit of the living God, not on tablets of stone but on tablets of human hearts. (2 Corinthians 3:3 ESV)

The only way we can finally make that jump is not only to see with our minds that there is solid evidence for the case of Christ, but we must also believe that he is love incarnate and that we do not have to fear the cliff because we will meet his love on the other side—perfect love, perfect love that casts out all fears.

The song by For King & Country, *Middle of Your Heart*, sums this up beautifully:

> So take me to the middle of Your heart
> Lead me to wherever Your love starts
> To a new day dawning
> To the place You are
> And if You want to take me over the edge
> I'll let you 'cause Your love is where I'll land
> Wanna be right where You are,
> In the middle of Your heart
>
> This is what I believe
> That if I give you my everything
> I will become who I was really born to be

We cannot fully become who we were born to be without taking that leap. We can do good things, we can be nice people, we can grow, we can be generous, but we will never find out who we were destined to be if we never take the leap. I realize this is a hard message for some. I have been reminded that not everyone is ready to hear that without falling over the cliff into the middle of the heart of Yeshua Adonai, the Creator of the universe and God of the angel armies, we will always be limited. Yet if it is true, then it is not my message to dilute. I do a disservice to everyone, including myself, not to state this message as clearly as I possibly can.

God did not come to earth to lay out a proof, to make bad people good, or to help people be a better version of themselves. God came to earth for something so much bigger and more radical. He came to show us what truth, grace, and love look like in real action. He came to make dead people live. How could I ever consider watering down that message to something people are more comfortable with?

Make no mistake. There is an active force that wants to be sure no one hears this daring and dangerous message. There is an active force that wants this to be kept fringe, secret, scorned. There is an active force that wants to keep you from believing it could be true. Do not assume for one moment that the ground is neutral. The truth is fighting to break into your life and heart. And there is a force that will stop at nothing to keep you from hearing it. And if it can't keep you from hearing, then it will convince you that it's all a crazy dream.

The truth is there is a better kingdom than the one the dark forces have set up here on earth. We were made to walk with God in the garden, to work the ground and create, to grow good things, to love and be loved, to find satisfaction in work that we love— everything went wrong thousands of years ago. Yet God is still in the business of trying to show us we can have it all but only with him at the center.

# Chapter 14

# Getting It Wrong

I n earlier pages of this book, I describe how God first began the process of blessing the world by choosing a man with faith and told him, "Follow me, and I will make your descendants a people and bless the world through them." Abraham took a giant step and walked away from what he knew to answer this call. The nation of Israel was born from that step of faith, and it is a massive people group today spread over the entire world. That man took the leap without all the answers in advance and changed the trajectory of the entire planet.

We all have a calling that can change the trajectory of the planet. God doesn't do small callings. Each one of us has a massive role to play in saving the world from darkness. It may not seem that way from our limited perspective, that does not mean it isn't so.

I hope someday to be able to revel in the amazement of the ripple effect of something that seemed insignificant that changed someone's day, heart, or life that in turn changed someone's day, heart, or life and so on like a light that spreads in the dark one candle at a time. I am also glad I do not know these details today because I'm susceptible to falling into pride, exaggerating my importance in changing the world. And the temptation is great to think I'm the important one. I can be quick to forget that I don't even know what I'm doing most of the time and am certain to cause wreckage if I'm not submitted to

God's plan. It's not my actions that are changing the world, it is the fact that I've submitted my actions to obey God's direction because he has the master plan. I am vital and important, and I'm loved completely but left to my own devices. I'm often a train wreck!

Then again, so were the chosen people. In time, the nation of Israel that God began from one man and woman of great faith, a couple who seemed too old to have a family, finally had a son. And over time, that small beginning grew into huge numbers while in Egypt. They went first as family of honored guests, and then over generations, as they carried the favor of God, the Egyptians in power grew concerned. (Watch for this in your own life!) The powers of the land, out of fear, tried to contain them with slavery and bondage.

Moses was another man called by God to participate in a mighty calling. He was the one famous for bringing that massive nation out of slavery. Moses tried to do this in his own way and his own time when he killed an Egyptian guard and got it wrong. He had the right idea. But in trying to do it with his own human vision, he was an abject failure who ended up on the run. It's okay. We regularly mess things up, and God still has a plan. After forty years in his own personal wilderness being shaped and humbled, God, in the exact right time, brought Moses back to the Egyptian palace this time as an outsider.

Following God almost always means you become an outsider in some way because the darkness does not understand or accept the light. I'd rather be an outsider in the wilderness with God than in the palace without him!

Moses gets a second chance. And when it is done God's way, it will succeed. Moses leads the biggest freedom march in the history of the world. Yet out of slavery often means getting into the wilderness first. We might be able to get out of Egypt, but it takes longer for God to get the Egypt out of us. This is another season to watch for in your own life. The trials of the wilderness teach us survival, strength, and above all, dependence on God for everything.

God brought them into a land where evil and darkness had been spreading. (They were famous for sacrificing babies by burning to the local god, Molech.) And one small victory at a time, they won the land for good, and their one job was to live out this kingdom of light and show the other nations how living in God's ways are better. They would be the proof to the world around them. He gave his people in the wilderness the law that was based on this precept: love. First, love God with your heart and mind and spirit. And from this love, then love those around you who God also loves and made in his own image. Your neighbor, regardless if you like her or not, is loved by God, and you must treat her with dignity, respect and love and care for each other.

Unfortunately, the nation, full of humans that get things wrong, failed at this over time.

> How the faithful city has become a whore, she who was full of justice! Righteousness lodged in her but now murderers. Your silver has become dross, your best wine mixed with water. Your princes are rebels and companions of thieves. Everyone loves a bribe and runs after gifts. They do not bring justice to the fatherless, and the widow's cause does not come to them." (Isaiah 1:21–23 ESV)

> Learn to do good; seek justice, correct oppression; bring justice to the fatherless, plead the widow's cause. Come now, let us reason together, says the Lord: though your sins are like scarlet, they shall be as white as snow; though they are red like crimson, they shall become like wool. Isaiah 1:17–18 ESV

Just like Moses, just like me, Israel failed at this over and over. Humans are imperfect, and we get free choice; we have a tendency to choose poorly. Still God never gave up on the people who he loves. And no matter how many times we fail, he still gives us the opportunity to choose again. It is obvious that God isn't afraid of our failures. He wants to have connection with us. He wants our hearts and minds and love. He wants us to choose better, to choose him. He's willing to do things the messy and inefficient way. He doesn't merely want to get something done; he wants us. Thus, he keeps allowing humans to screw things up, fixing them, and hoping we will choose him instead.

When I reflect on this amazing fact, I also see that the worse the circumstances we create when we get it wrong, the more amazing the glory that comes from God, turning it around and making it right. The darker the darkness, the brighter the light shines.

After years of the chosen people, getting it wrong, God, in his own time, came himself. This saving of all of humanity was that important. He was the only one able to get the job done completely without getting anything wrong. He came to be the way. He was the flawless example of perfection we could never achieve, but it's so much more than that. He promised it would be different from then on. After he left, he would send the spirit of God to live in and through us. We would be given the power to defeat evil.

A lesson I have been slow to understand is why then does it seem so often that darkness has its way even when women and men of great faith who carry that light are involved? If we have the power, then why do people still die? Why is there still injustice? Why do innocents still suffer even when they are bringing the kingdom power to these situations?

I have limited understanding as a human, but I think of a recent fictional account of a war spy story where a compromised politician was found out. One high level player in the meeting called to immediately arrest and take out the compromised diplomat, but a wiser voice won the meeting with the suggestion that leaving the compromised actor in play but now with knowledge of such, there was much greater value in either feeding misinformation or possibly a counteroffer to create a double agent. This kind of understanding in war situations reminds me that sometimes the short-sighted choices seem good, but a longer-range vision may leave evil in play for a time to accomplish a greater victory.

Without question, the greatest story in human history allowed evil to have a temporary triumph in torturing and killing Yeshua. But it was with a much greater goal on the horizon. When God allows for a temporary suffering or a death in our lives, one thing we cannot say is that he is putting us through anything he didn't volunteer for while he lived. And we can forget the notion that bad things don't happen to good people. The worst thing happened to the very best person to ever live. But we do stand in the assurance that now, death is defeated. And human death is not the worst thing that can happen to someone if they have chosen the one who overcame death.

The kingdom of God is at hand already. It is in the transition phase of here but not fully yet. What an exciting time to be a human! Darkness and evil have been taking over the globe. Terrible attacks have been played out on those following God's ways. Violence is their way, and they've been at it for centuries. And then God appears to us and brings not only by example but now by force!

> From the days of John the Baptist until now
> the kingdom of heaven has suffered violence, and
> the violent take it by force. (Matthew 11:12 ESV)

Hold on!

We get this wrong too! This is not force against people but force against the powers of darkness. If we do not understand the concepts of chapter 5 that we are freedom fighters but our enemy is the dark spiritual forces, not each other, we will do great harm to the very cause we are supposed to be championing. We are called to put on our spiritual armor and learn to fight on our knees in prayer and also submission to God's ways. He is the commander who can see more moves ahead than we can, and he is able to direct us expertly, often in ways that make little sense to our ground view vantage point.

Our only hope is a life of submission. No matter how much we get wrong, if we are submitting constantly to God's will, he can sort it out and bring glory. This does not mean we don't have responsibility to try to get it right. We have lots of instruction directly from God on how to make good choices and bring blessing to our lives and the world around us. We do know right and wrong.

Unfortunately, not all our decisions fall into that obvious category. Most of us do not train wreck over things so plain as murder, theft, and lying. Sometimes choosing who to date and marry are clear because there are huge red flags. But sometimes people try to make a good choice and end up blindsided by things they couldn't know. No one can guess what twenty-five years of marriage will do to a couple, and sometimes things go wrong in ways we can't control. The world takes loved ones in accidents or illness, and a future can change in moments or days.

I am convinced that we cannot get things so wrong that we end up with God's plan $B$ for our life or plan $C$ or $D$. I took some time to realize an underlying belief in my own life was that I had messed things up so badly that I was definitely way off course for God's best plan for my life. This was a deep belief that I would have said I did not hold, but the Holy Spirit gradually revealed this in a way I could not dispute it. I did believe I had messed up my life with poor choices. And now in my forties, the best I could do was turn it over to God and let him make a decent second or third chance in my life.

For any of you who feel like they are on plan $X$, $Y$, or even $Z$ for your life, I submit the story of Saul turned Paul. Most of us know the story of the Christian killer met by Jesus on the road to Damascus who saw the light and turned his life around to be one of the major authors of our Bible texts and super-Christian extraordinaire. We look at his story and tell each other, "See, you cannot mess up your life bad enough that God cannot use you." However, is this our only lesson from the story?

Didn't people lose their lives because of Saul, the Christian-hating pharisee's zealous persecution? Was God's perfect plan for Saul's life missed because Saul didn't see the light sooner? Was Saul/Paul's life his plan $B$?

I submit the question above all of these: Was God unable to get to Saul sooner?

My closer reading of this story is that everything happened right on time for Saul to make the change to Paul the apostle on the road to Damascus. God could have revealed himself to the man at any moment. I suggest that the great writer and early church leader was in his only and exact plan *A* for his life just as you are living in the only plan for your life there ever would be. Without Paul's story in the New Testament, we may forever wonder if there's a sin we could have committed that is too great for God to use our lives powerfully. As terrible as it is that people had to die in order for us to know this truth, I am also grateful.

This doesn't mean yours and my poor life choices (killing Christians would be an example) didn't hurt others and cause pain in the world. This doesn't mean we don't feel the need for repentance and sorrow for the damage that came when we ran from God. It does however mean that once we turn from these ways, and we begin to live a life submitted to God's plan that we can walk forward in the assurance that we are not in some sorry, second rate life that will never be as good as what God had originally intended for us. This lie quietly operated in the background of my life as I saw two broken marriages and an uncertain future. There was a place in me certain that I could never have the life I was meant to have if I'd have gotten it right in the first place.

I had to first realize this lie was at work, and that may have been the biggest hurdle of all. It did surprise me to realize there could be lies operating deep down that I would say I do not believe. This is something the Holy Spirit is really good at, and he does it gently over time as we are able to face them. Another name for him is the spirit of truth, and facing the truth within us is invaluable for growing into a force of good.

The next step is to fight lies with truth. The truth is that God is bigger than everything and everyone around me. The truth is that other people are not in charge of my future. God has the controls, and there is no evil plan that can override God's plans for my life and the promise that they are plans to prosper me, to give me a future and a hope.

> For I know the plans I have for you, declares
> the Lord, plans for welfare and not for evil, to give
> you a future and a hope. (Jeremiah 29:11 ESV)

The next truth that applies here is the promise that everything will be used for my good, if I am called to God's purposes. I am called and also have chosen to participate in God's plan.

> And we know that for those who love God,
> all things work together for good, for those who
> are called according to his purpose. (Romans
> 8:28 ESV)

When I think through and pray about these promises in light of the fears that my life will always be some kind of second-best alternate plan, then I see the example of Saul turned Paul and how he was used powerfully because of his life history not despite it, I begin in my mind fighting against the lies in my heart.

It always takes time for the truth in my mind to penetrate my heart. But in time, as I allow the Holy Spirit to work, my heart does change. The truth sets me free, and I can walk with confidence that my past has prepared me for my future perfectly, and I am in the center of God's plan for my life and for the lives I'll impact as he puts me in contact with others.

No matter what you have done to get it wrong, God is working it all—every single poor decision and every single pain and every single circumstance. All of it is the promise that goes into the tapestry of your life that he weaves into something beautiful to bring glory to him and blessing to us. Here today, we see an underside of knotted threads and colors in lines that don't make sense, but someday in eternity, it will be turned over to reveal a thing of extreme beauty.

It's like the master Gardner who takes us wherever we are and turns over our barren soil to uncover the riches and depth only he can nurture. And from the desert we were, he makes a garden. He grows his roses on our once barren soul. It isn't about what we offer or how great our past lines up no matter who we are, it's about being loved by the Creator and given the amazing place of daughter instead of prisoner and outcast.

*Who Am I* by Needtobreathe

White lights and desperation
Hard times and conversation
No one should ever love me like you do

Sometimes my bad decisions
Define my false suspicions
No one should ever love me like you do

While I'm on this road, you take my hand
Somehow you really love who I really am
I push you away, still you won't let go

You grow your roses on my barren soul
Who am I, who am I, who am I
To be loved by you

# About the Author

J aime Hope McArdle is a violin teacher, performer, horsemanship coach, and blog writer in the rural mountains of Virginia. Since childhood, she filled volumes of journals, processing the influences that have shaped her life and has a particular interest in the unseen spiritual underpinnings of everyday events. After completing a master's of music in violin performance from the San Francisco Conservatory of Music, Jaime worked in the Bay Area a few years then, in 2007, traded the city life for one of the least-populated areas in the state of Virginia to work at the Garth Newel Music Center. Here she founded the Allegheny Mountain String Project, a privately funded youth music education program and is adjunct professor of violin and chamber music at Washington and Lee University.

In a county with no stoplights and 85 percent national forest, Jaime fell in love with horses and has two mares: Khaleesi, a locally bred mare she started as a four-year-old and competes in equine endurance events, and Wyoming, a wild mustang who is constantly teaching her more of the nature of horses. Working with horses inspired her to begin a blog (greento100.com) to chronicle how the process of starting and training a horse has influenced her view of the world. Recently, she began the blog "Enter the Whisper" (www. jaimemcardle.wixsite.com/EnterTheWhisper) to share conversations she has with the whisper in the spirit.

As a Sunday school kid with a prayer warrior mom, Jaime spent most of her life on the run from God to seek her own way. After two failed marriages, she came to the end of her own road and finally challenged the Creator to make himself known in a way she could understand. He led her one day at a time from being a prisoner of her own self into a freedom to go beyond outside circumstances, and her life has never been the same. She continues to champion this freedom to anyone seeking it and is also deeply concerned for those who are physically in bondage to human trafficking and slavery today.

CPSIA information can be obtained
at www.ICGtesting.com
Printed in the USA
BVHW051504280622
640817BV00008B/253